A-Z
SOCIOLOGY
Workbook

A-Z

SOCIOLOGY

Workbook

Tony Lawson
Joan Garrod

Hodder & Stoughton

A MEMBER OF THE HODDER HEADLINE GROUP

Orders: please contact Bookpoint Ltd, 130 Milton Park, Abingdon,
Oxon OX14 4SB. Telephone: (44) 01235 827720, Fax: (44) 01235 400454.
Lines are open from 9.00–6.00, Monday to Saturday, with a 24 hour message
answering service. Email address: orders@bookpoint.co.uk

British Library Cataloguing in Publication Data
A catalogue record for this title is available from the British Library

ISBN 0 340 799838

First published 2001
Impression number   10 9 8 7 6 5 4 3 2 1
Year   2005 2004 2003 2002 2001

Cover artwork by Alan Nanson
Typeset by Florence Production Ltd, Stoodleigh, Devon
Printed in Great Britain for Hodder & Stoughton Education,
a division of Hodder Headline Plc, 338 Euston Road, London NW1 3BH
by Martins the Printers, Berwick-upon-Tweed

Contents

To Tom Whiteside
Teacher, mentor, friend

How to use this book

This book is organised alphabetically by concept. Each of the concepts has an exercise to help you develop and test your understanding of that concept and, in many cases, other related concepts.

One way of using the book is to decide which topic area you are going to revise, and use the list below to see which exercises you should do. Remember, though, that some concepts are useful for more than one topic area, so use your text book and handouts to see whether there are any others that would be helpful. Another way is to use the book to help you with your understanding of particular concepts that you find difficult or unclear. Don't forget that the *A–Z Sociology Handbook* is a very useful source for the definition and explanation of concepts. Try not to look at the answers in the Workbook until you have attempted to do the exercises, or you will lose much of the benefit that this book can give you.

Sociological theory

Action
Conflict
Consensus
Determinism
Feminism
Functionalism
Interactionism
Marxism
Meta–narrative
Modernity
Perspectives
Positivism
Post–modernity
Social change
Social facts
Social order
Social policy
Social structure
Sociology as a science
Theory

Sociological methods

Content analysis
Ethical issues
Experiment
Hawthorne effect
Hypothesis
Interview
Objectivity
Observation
Official statistics
Practical constraints
Primary data
Qualitative data
Quantitative data
Questionnaire
Reliability
Response rate
Sampling
Secondary data
Subjectivity
Validity

Families and households

Childhood
Cohabitation
Conjugal roles
Core functions of the family
Death of the family
Divorce
Domestic labour
Extended family
Family fit
Family size
Family structure
Household
Lone-parent families
Loss of family functions
Marriage
Nuclear family
Patriarchy
Socialisation
Symmetrical family
Universality of the family

Health

Artefact explanation
Body
Disability
Health
Health care
iatrogenesis
Illness
Infant mortality rate
Life chances
Medical model
Medical technology
Medicalisation
Mental illness
Mortality rate
National Health
Primary health care
Private medicine
Reproductive technologies
Sick role
Social selection explanation

Mass media

Agenda-setting
Allocative control
Conglomeration
Decoding
Empty bucket theory
Gate-keepers
Headlining
Mass media
Mass society
Media effects
Media industries
Media representations
Mediation
Moral panic
News values
Operational control
Opinion leaders
Selective exposure
Signification
Text

Education

Allocation process
Clash of cultures
Classroom interaction
Compensatory education
Comprehensivisation
Correspondence principle
Cultural capital
Cultural reproduction
Curriculum
Educational standards
Equality of opportunity
Hidden curriculum
Home background
Language codes
National curriculum
New vocationalism
Parental attitudes to education
Secondary socialisation
Underachievement
Educational standards

Wealth, poverty and welfare

Absolute poverty
Collectivism
Culture of poverty
Cycle of poverty
Feminisation of poverty
Income
Index of deprivation
Inequality
Inheritance
Poverty line
Relative poverty
Situational constraints
Subjective poverty
Taxation
Underclass
Victim-blaming
Wealth
Welfare
Welfare dependency
Welfare state

Work and leisure

Affluent workers
Alienation
Anomie
Automation
Bureaucracy
Consumption
De-skilling
Domestic economy
Feminisation of work
Formal economy
Human Relations School
Industrial conflict
Leisure
Logic of industrialism
Scientific management
Strike statistics
Technological determinism
Unemployment
Work
Work satisfaction

Power and politics

Authority
Cheque-book voting
Democracy
Hegemony
Ideology
Legitimation
New Social Movements
Pluralism
Political culture
Political identification
Political participation
Political party
Politics
Power
Pressure groups
Problem of order
Re-alignment theories
Ruling class
State
Unitary elite theory

Religion

Church
Church attendance statistics
Demystification
Denomination
Ecumenicalism
Fundamentalism
Golden Age of Religion
Individuation
Liberation theology
New Christian Right
New Religious Movements
Profane
Protestant ethic thesis
Quantum theory of religion
Religion
Religiosity
Religious observance
Sacred
Sect
Secularisation

World sociology

Aid
Colonialism
Dependency theory
Development
Dual economy thesis
First world
Five stages of economic growth
Globalisation
Green revolution
Industrialisation
Metropolis
Modernisation theory
Newly industrialising countries
North-South
Third world
Tiger economies
Trans-national companies
Under-development
Urbanisation
World system theory

Crime and deviance

Crime
Crimes of the powerful
Crimes without victims
Critical criminology
Culture structure
Dark figure of crime
Deviance
Differential Association theory
Drift
Folk devils
Juvenile delinquency
Labelling theory
New deviancy theory
Self-fulfilling prophecy
Social construction
Social control
Social order
Street crime
Suicide
Victim studies

Stratification and differentiation

Age-set
Caste
Class boundaries debate
Class structure
Embourgeoisement
Indicators of class
Life chances
Middle class
Occupational structure
Persistence theories
Prestige
Problem of consciousness
Proletarianisation
Social class
Social closure
Social mobility
Stratification
Upper class
Working class

Socialisation, culture and identity

Age
Culture
Discourse
Empowerment
Ethnicity
Gender
Gender codes
Hyper-reality
Identity
Identity construction
Mass culture
Modernity
Norms
Other
Post-modernity
Self
Status
Sub-culture
Surveillance
Values

A–Z Questions

Identify and explain one criticism which could be made of the view that absolute poverty exists only in some developing societies and not in Western industrial societies.

....

....

....

....

Action

Complete the table below by filling in the missing words against each of the numbers.

	Action (interactionism)	System (structural functionalism)
Basic elements of social life	The 1 .... of individuals.	Social 2 ....
Social reality	Emerges from the ways in which individuals define 3	Is 4 .... to individuals.
Roles	Individuals interpret and 5 .... their own roles based on what is learned during the process of 6	Individuals conform to role 7 .... learned during the process of socialisation.
The role of the sociologist	Sociologists must try to understand people's 8 .... in terms of their 9 .... meaning.	Sociologists must try to understand how people's behaviour is constrained by social 10 ....

external   actions   systems   socialisation   expectations
subjective   situations   structures   actions   create

1

Affluent workers

Distinguish between the following pairs of terms, which are associated with Goldthorpe and Lockwood's 'affluent workers'.

1 **(a)** Affluent working class

....

....

....

....

(b) Instrumental working class

....

....

....

....

2 **(a)** Embourgeoisement

....

....

....

....

(b) Proletarianisation

....

....

....

....

3 **(a)** Privatised working class

....

....

....

....

(b) Traditional working class

....

....

....

....

4 **(a)** Incorporation thesis

....

....

....

....

(b) Immiseration thesis

....

....

....

....

5 **(a)** Aristocracy of labour

....

....

....

....

(b) Lumpenproletariat

....

....

....

....

Age

Offer a definition of each of these concepts associated with the sociology of age, giving examples.

1 Age dependency ....
....
....
....
....

2 Gerontocracy ....
....
....
....
....

3 Generation
....
....
....
....

4 Third age
....
....
....
....

5 Youth subculture
....
....
....
....

Age-set

Give three characteristics of an age-set.

1 ....
....
....
....

2 ....
....
....
....

3 ....
....
....
....

Agenda-setting

Which of the following groups, concerned with the production of newspapers, have the potential to set the agenda of public debate about issues? In the final column, give an explanation for your decision, which illustrates how the social actor does or does not agenda-set.

Social actor	Power to set the agenda?	Explanation
1 Copy typist	Yes No	
2 Journalist	Yes No	
3 Editor	Yes No	
4 Printer	Yes No	
5 Owner	Yes No	

Aid

Place the following concepts concerned with aid to poor countries in the appropriate perspective column, explaining what is meant by each one. Complete the table by suggesting one criticism of each perspective's view of aid.

dependency culture   imperialism by the back door   intermediate technology

	1 Marxist	2 Social Democratic	3 New Right
(A) Concept			
(B) Explanation			
(C) Criticism			

Alienation

From the following description of life in a factory, highlight the phrases that illustrate the following dimensions of alienation, indicating which dimension is which.

1 isolation   **2 mechanisation**   **3 meaninglessness**

4 specialisation   **5 powerlessness**   **6 self-estrangement**

The factory is organised into separate units, characterised by different machines to carry out different functions. All the workers are allocated to particular machines to carry out their work. They have no choice over which machine they are attached to as this is a management function. Each worker is given a specific machine to work with and has to learn the tasks associated with that machine and no other. Every worker is therefore expected to focus on their own tasks and ignore other aspects of the productive process. To try to ensure that workers keep their mind on the task in hand, management has used the machinery to separate out individual workers, so that any communication between them is difficult. In these circumstances, most workers have little commitment to work and just want to get on with their job and get out of the factory as quickly as possible at night, back to their families or social lives.

Allocation process

Match each of the following concepts to the appropriate definition from the list below.

(a) allocation process

(b) labelling

(c) meritocracy

(d) self-fulfilling prophecy

(e) streaming

1   A process in which certain characteristics, often negative ones, are attached to particular pupils or groups of pupils.

2   An organisational device for separating students into groups according to their perceived ability.

3   The ways in which pupils are categorised, sorted and certificated by the education system to produce different types of worker for the economy.

4   A statement or a belief about a predicted outcome which, by subsequent actions, helps to bring about that outcome.

5   A social system in which rewards are allocated on the basis of worth and achievement rather than on ascriptive factors such as class or gender.

Allocative control

Answer the following questions about allocative control in organisations.

1 Which position in an organisation commands allocative control?

....

....

....

....

2 Does allocative control refer to strategic or operational planning?

....

....

....

....

3 What do you think is the most important aspect of allocative control?

....

....

....

....

4 Who will be more influential in determining allocations – the senior management or the Board of Directors?

....

....

....

....

5 Suggest two specific ways in which subordinate members of organisations may experience the effects of allocative control.

....

....

....

....

Anomie

Match up the concepts to the sociologist who is most identified with them.

Anomie

Ideal type   Durkheim

Exploitation

Verstehen

Rational action   Marx

Forces of production

Organic solidarity

Interdependence of inter-related parts   Weber

Alienation

Artefact explanation

Match the explanation of social class health inequalities to the appropriate label.

Explanation of social class health inequalities	Label
1 People in the lower social class groups are not as 'health-conscious' and thus do not look after themselves as well as those in higher classes. These poor attitudes to health are then passed on to the next generation, thus perpetuating health inequalities.	**(A)** artefact explanation
2 Poorer health in the lower social classes is the result of a number of factors, most beyond the control of those affected. Such factors include poverty, dangerous working environments and high levels of stress and depression.	**(B)** natural/social selection explanation
3 Health inequalities are the result of misleading statistics or inappropriate definitions of social class. They are therefore not 'real'.	**(C)** structural/ material explanation
4 Poor health is a cause, rather than a result, of people being in lower social class groups. Being in poor health prevents them from achieving and maintaining higher-ranking jobs.	**(D)** behavioural/ cultural explanation

Authority

Indicate whether the people in the situations below should be described as wielding authority, power or both.

Situation	Authority	Power	Both
1 A teacher in a classroom			
2 Parents with their children			
3 A boss telling workers what to do			
4 A military dictator making laws			
5 A police officer arresting a suspect			
6 A prime minister chairing a cabinet meeting			

Automation

The impact of automated technologies on work has been argued to be immense, along many dimensions. Suggest ten potential effects on work and workers that might follow the introduction of automated technologies. Some of these may be contradictory.

1 ....

2 ....

3 ....

4 ....

5 ....

6 ....

7 ....

8 ....

9 ....

10 ....

Body

Fill in the gaps, using the words from the list below.

In sociology, the 'body' is viewed not simply as a **1** .... entity but as a **2** .... **3** .... At different times and in different **4** ...., the body has been regarded in different ways. Some groups regard it as a sacred vessel, to be kept **5** ...., while others see it as under constant attack, for example from evil **6** .... or magic spells. Foucault and other **7** .... – .... argue that people's conceptions of their body are influenced by **8** .... These define such things as appropriate or desirable **9** .... **10** ...., and also the best ways of keeping the body healthy. **11** .... argue that women in particular are subjected to strong **12** .... to achieve and maintain a desirable body. This has led to growing concern regarding the spread, particularly among teenage girls, of **13** .... **14** .... such as **15** .... and **16** .... **17** ....

post-modernists bulimia societies discourses disorders nervosa body pressures eating construct shape physical feminists pure social anorexia demons

Bureaucracy

Answer the following questions about bureaucracies and organisations.

1   Weber's model of bureaucracy is an example of his main methodological construct. What is this?

....

2   What type of organisation describes what actually goes on, rather than what is supposed to go on?

....

3   How did Gouldner describe those rules that actually operate in an organisation rather than the rule book?

....

4   Marxists argued that bureaucracies were efficient in controlling what?

....

5   Foucault argued that the focus of organisations in a post-modern society is what?

....

6   What did Ritzer call the strict rationalisation of products in a post-modern society?

....

7   When the rules of an organisation do not fulfil the goals of the organisation, they are said to be what?

....

8   What is it called when a small group controls a large organisation?

....

9   Burns and Stalker contrasted mechanistic organisations with what?

....

10   When an organisation controls individuals 24/7, they are called what?

....

Caste

Complete the table below by identifying whether the description fits a stratification system of caste, estate or class, or more than one of these.

Characteristic	Caste	Estate	Class
1 Has a set of legally defined rights and duties.			
2 Membership is ascribed.			
3 Based on the Hindu religion.			
4 Particularly associated with modern industrial societies.			
5 Particularly associated with feudal societies.			
6 Groups ranked according to a system of ritual purity.			
7 According to Marx, based on relationship to capitalist means of production.			
8 Main divisions: nobility, clergy and commoners.			
9 People grouped into five main divisions.			
10 Tends to be based on occupation.			
11 Members expected to marry within the group (endogamous).			
12 A hierarchical system of stratification.			
13 Elements of ascription, but movement from one group to another (achievement) possible.			

Cheque book voting

Write a brief paragraph about the significance of 'cheque book voting', using the following words, though not necessarily in the order given.

instrumental   taxation   public issues

private prosperity   opinion polls

....

....

....

....

....

Childhood

Explain in your own words what is meant by the following sentences.

1 Childhood has both chronological and social definition.

....

....

2 The state defines many of the roles and responsibilities of childhood.

....

....

3 Childhood is a relatively recent social construction.

....

....

4 The definition of childhood impacts upon the criminal justice system.

....

....

....

5 Biological maturity is no guarantee of social maturity.

....

....

15

Church

List five characteristics of a 'Church'.

1 ....

2 ....

3 ....

4 ....

5 ....

Church attendance statistics

State three criticisms which can be made of the use of church attendance statistics as a way of measuring the degree of religiosity in society.

1 ....

....

2 ....

....

3 ....

....

Clash of cultures

The following concepts refer to suggested explanations of the educational underachievement of certain children from ethnic minority groups. For each concept, write at least one criticism which has been made of it.

Concept	Criticism
1 Clash of cultures	....
2 Black box view	....
3 Language	....

Class boundaries debate

Identify and briefly explain a criticism which could be made of each of the following ways of dividing society into class groups.

1   Bourgeoisie/proletariat.

   ....

   ....

   ....

2   Upper, middle and working class.

   ....

   ....

   ....

3   The Registrar-General's five occupational class groups.

   ....

   ....

   ....

Class structure

Identify and briefly explain two ways in which the occupational class structure in Britain has changed since 1945.

1   ....

   ....

2   ....

   ....

Classroom interaction

Write a brief paragraph explaining why some sociologists have emphasised the importance of classroom interaction to an understanding of educational success and failure, using all the following terms, though not necessarily in the order in which they are given.

interactionist   negotiated process   peer group

negative stereotypes   meanings

Cohabitation

Distinguish between the following.

1 cohabitation marriage same sex couples

2 divorce marital breakdown separation

3 adoption fostering voluntary childlessness

Collectivism

Distinguish between 'collectivism' and 'individualism' in terms of the provision of welfare.

....

....

....

....

Colonialism

Write a paragraph about the 'legacy of colonialism', using the following terms/concepts.

history   language   customs   national boundaries

trading relationships   neo-colonialism   decolonisation

divide-and-rule   colonial powers   community of nations

....

....

....

....

....

....

....

....

....

....

....

Compensatory education

Fill in the blanks in the following piece, using the words from the list at the end.

The idea of 'culturally deprived' children originated in the **1** .... in the mid–1950s, and quickly became a popular way of 'explaining' the **2** .... of many children from **3** .... working-class and **4** .... **5** .... families. The suggestion was that the children's **6** .... **7** .... was culturally deficient, and that they were thus **8** .... when they arrived at school. The Federal Government's 'War on Poverty' launched in 1963 emphasised **9** .... as a major means of improving the condition of the poor. Several **10** .... **11** .... programmes were developed, including Operation **12** .... **13** .... It is **14** .... to assess the value of such programmes. They resulted in an initial spurt in the children's **15** .... scores, but the **16** .... phenomenon soon became apparent, where children who were not in the programmes also showed an **17** ....

There have been many criticisms of the ideas of **18** .... **19** .... and compensatory education. One is that it is not true that some groups lack '**20** ....'. What is being referred to is a particular set of values associated with the **21** .... **22** .... Again, to suggest that poverty and educational failure result from inadequate **23** .... ignores the underlying **24** .... causes of poverty. A belief in cultural deprivation may lead teachers to set low **25** .... for some groups of children, leading to a **26** .... – .... **27** ....

background   catch-up   class   compensatory

cultural   culture   deprivation   difficult

disadvantaged   education   education   ethnic   failure

Head   home   improvement   IQ   lower   middle

minority   prophecy   self-fulfilling   standards   Start

structural   United States   upbringing

Comprehensivisation

Give two reasons which could be made in favour of, and two reasons against, the comprehensivisation of secondary schools.

Reasons in favour	Reasons against
1..	1.. ....
2..	2.. ....

Conflict

Complete the following sentences by inserting the missing words.

1 Conflict theories developed as a reaction to the functionalists' emphasis on
....

2 Conflicts are seen as primarily arising over .... and ....
resources.

3 Marx saw the fundamental conflict in society between two groups, the ....
and the ....

4 More recent writers such as Dahrendorf have pointed out that conflict in today's society
is not just between .... groups.

5 A major criticism of conflict theory is its inability to explain the degree of
.... in societies.

Conglomeration

Attach the correct concept to the definition by drawing a line between them.

1 Conglomeration	**(A)** Where an industry becomes increasingly dominated by a small number of large companies, In the media, this has a global dimension.	2 Diversification
(B) Where an organisation, originally based, for example, in the media industry, takes over firms in related areas, so diluting its original area of interest.	**(C)** Where several companies from different sectors of industry are brought together in a single overarching company. Media companies, for example, may link to leisure industries.	
3 Concentration		

Conjugal roles

In each of the following dimensions of family life, describe what a segregated conjugal role household and a joint conjugal role household might look like. Then, write a paragraph on how these descriptions offer a stereotyped view of families in the past and present.

Dimension of family life	(A) Segregated conjugal roles	(B) Joint conjugal roles
I Power/decision making		
2 Domestic division of labour		
3 Responsibility for childcare		
4 Relationships with rest of the family		
5 Social life		

Consensus

Explain the difference between consensus and hegemony.

....

....

....

....

....

Consumption

Sociologists have become increasingly interested in issues of consumption. Write a paragraph on why this is the case, using all of the concepts listed below in as few sentences as possible, in the order that they are given.

consumption   leisure   leisure society

social class   identities   social indicator   life-styles

postmodern   shopping

....

....

....

....

....

....

....

Content analysis

Fill in the missing blanks by choosing an appropriate concept from your **A–Z Sociology Handbook.**

Content analysis is used by sociologists to examine **1** ...., whether they are written or visual. The sociologist has to suspend their **2** .... about the subject of the piece being analysed and adopt an objective approach. This may be done in either of two ways. The first is to adopt a

3 .... approach to content analysis, where words, phrases or amount of coverage are counted. For example, in a content analysis of newspapers, the number of column inches given over to different **4** .... might be counted. The main criticism here is that, while it might appear to be

5 ...., the significance of the numbers still has to be explained by the sociologist. The second way is to suspend the **6** .... and offer a deeper reading of the material. Some sociologists argue that by

7 .... the material in this way, for example by pointing out the connections between the material and other cultural references, the essential intertextuality of cultural forms is established. The main criticism here is that the sociologist cannot avoid subjectivity in this situation and that it leads therefore to

8 ...., where no one interpretation is privileged over any other.

Core functions of the family

Identify which of the following are core functions of the family and which are minor.

1 Providing primary health care for ill members of the family.
2 Providing a trade for younger members of the family.
3 Providing the young with the values and norms of society.
4 Providing an opportunity for expressing religious belief.
5 Providing society with the next generation.
6 Providing food and shelter for members.
7 Providing work for members.
8 Providing for the sexual and emotional needs of members.

Write a paragraph on why the minor functions have declined in importance over time.

Core functions	Minor functions

Correspondence principle

Below are five aspects of the correspondence principle in schools. For each one, give an example showing how this operates in schools. Then give three criticisms which could be made of the concept of the correspondence principle.

Aspect	Example
1 Education is a direct preparation for people's future role in the workplace.	
2 Schools operate with a system of rewards and punishments.	
3 Middle-class children are likely to have different educational experiences from those of working-class children.	
4 Middle-class children receive an education which prepares them for managerial type jobs rather than manual jobs.	
5 The education of working-class children emphasises obedience and discipline to prepare them for subordinate roles in the workplace.	

Criticisms of the concept of the correspondence principle.

1 ....

....

2 ....

....

3 ....

....

Crime

For each of the following activities, identify a time, or place, or context in which it might be legal and another in which it might be illegal.

Activity	(a) Legal	(b) Illegal
1 Swearing in public		
2 Abortion		
3 Drinking alcohol in a pub		
4 Smoking a cigarette		
5 Killing a human being		
6 Growing long hair		
7 Wearing no clothes		
8 Punching a person		
9 Killing animals		

Crimes of the powerful

Circle the odd one out in each sequence of three. Give a reason for your decision.

1 (a) Crimes of the powerful	(b) Occupational crime	(c) Corporate crime

Reason: ....

....

....

....

....

....

2 (a) Corporate crime	(b) Professional crime	(c) Occupational crime

Reason: ....

....

....

....

....

....

3 (a) Crimes of the powerful	(b) State crime	(c) White-collar crime

Reason: ....

....

....

....

....

Crimes without victims

Crimes without victims are those illegal activities in which all participants are consenting adults, who do not believe that a crime has been committed. Answer the following set of questions about crimes without victims.

1 Give three examples of crimes without victims.

(a) ....
....
(b) ....
....
(c) ....
....

2 For each of your examples, suggest a reason why the state may view it as criminal activity.

(a) ....
....
(b) ....
....
(c) ....
....

3 For each of your examples, give a reason why the perpetrators may not view their activity as criminal.

(a) ....
....
(b) ....
....
(c) ....
....

4 What do sociologists suggest is the reason why the state continues to criminalise such activity?

(a) ....
....
(b) ....
....
(c) ....
....

Critical criminology

Complete the following unfinished sentences about critical criminology and Marxist theories of crime and deviance. The first letter of the last word has been given to help you.

1 Critical criminology sees the main cause of crime as c.................................

2 Critical criminology sees society's main value as that of i.................................

3 Critical criminology argues that society encourages people to be a.................................

4 Critical criminology focuses mainly on crimes of p.................................

5 Critical criminology has been criticised for ignoring crime under s.................................

Cultural capital

State whether each of the following is an example of 'cultural capital' or not, explaining your answer.

Feature	Yes/No	Explanation
1 Home computer		....
2 Designer clothes		....
3 Wide vocabulary		....
4 Self-confidence		....
5 Large amount of pocket money		....

Cultural reproduction

State which one of the three statements below is a correct definition of cultural reproduction. Identify the concepts described by the remaining two.

(a) A situation in which one group imposes its culture on another.

....
....

(b) The process whereby social relationships of superordination and subordination in the class structure are recreated in each successive generation.

....
....
....
....

(c) A view that much working-class under-achievement in education is a result of a mismatch between working-class culture and the culture of the school.

....
....
....
....

Culture

Distinguish between:

1 (a) Primary identifier		**(b)** Secondary identifier
....		....
2 (a) High culture		**(b)** Popular culture
....		....
3 (a) Cultural conformity		**(b)** Cultural diversity
....		....
4 (a) Post-figurative culture	**(b)** Configurative culture	**(c)** Pre-figurative culture
....	....	....
5 (a) Hegemonic culture		**(b)** Subordinate culture
....		....

33

Culture of poverty

(A) *Complete the following by giving a brief explanation showing how each characteristic of the 'culture of poverty' might work to prevent someone escaping from poverty.*

Characteristic	Explanation
1 Fatalism	
2 Dependency	
3 Apathy	
4 Despair	
5 Immediate gratification	

(B) *Identify three criticisms which could be made of the concept of the culture of poverty.*

1 ....

2 ....

3 ....

Culture structure

Distinguish between the following concepts, associated with Merton's idea of a culture structure.

1 **(a)** Institutional means

....

....

....

....

(b) Cultural goals

....

....

....

....

2 **(a)** Mode of adaption

....

....

....

....

(b) Conformity

....

....

....

....

3 **(a)** Innovator

....

....

....

....

(b) Ritualist

....

....

....

....

4 **(a)** Retreatist

....

....

....

....

(b) Rebel

....

....

....

....

Curriculum

Distinguish between the following terms.

(a) The curriculum

....

....

....

(b) The hidden curriculum

....

....

....

(c) The National Curriculum

....

....

....

(d) An ethnocentric curriculum

....

....

....

(e) Extra-curricular activities

....

....

....

Cycle of poverty

Insert the statements below into the appropriate boxes to illustrate the cycle of poverty.

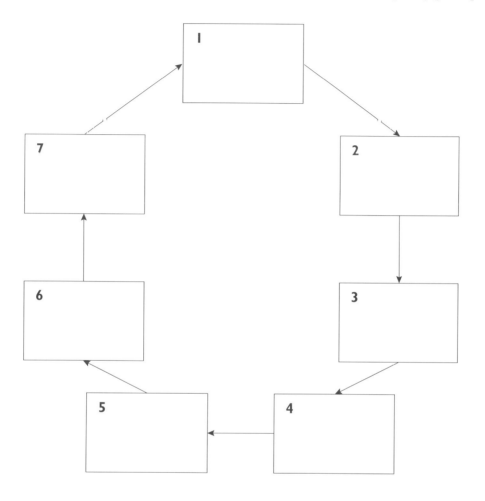

(a) Few educational qualifications

(b) Poor health throughout childhood

(c) Becomes a parent

(d) Unhealthy living accommodation and poor diet

(e) Child born into poor family

(f) Unemployment or low-paid job

(g) Frequent absences from school

Dark figure of crime

For each of the following reasons for the dark figure of crime, provide an appropriate example of a criminal activity likely to be associated with it.

1   The victim is unaware that a crime has
    been committed. ....

2   Victimless crimes, where both parties to
    an illegal action are consenting. ....

3   The victim does not believe that the
    police will catch the criminal. ....

4   The victim fears the personal consequences
    for the perpetrator if the crime is reported. ....

5   The victim fears being subject to public
    humiliation during the trial of the perpetrator. ....

6   The victim feels that the seriousness of
    the crime does not warrant its reporting. ....

Death of the family

The idea that the family is dying suggests that there is a major decline in the importance of the family in modern societies. Give three arguments in favour of this view and three arguments against.

1 Arguments in favour of the death of the family	2 Arguments against the death of the family
(a)	(a) ....
(b)	(b) ....
(c)	(c) ....

Decoding

Insert an appropriate sociological concept into the following sentences.

1 Decoding is the process whereby an .... interprets the messages of a media product.

2 When producers of media messages are composing their work, they have ideas they wish to communicate to their readers, which are .... in the way the content is presented.

3 There are many different types of media products, which regardless of their differences have messages to be decoded. To indicate this commonality, sociologists call all such messages ....

4 When readers decode media messages, they may interpret them differently from the .... of the producers.

5 Because readers of media messages bring with them their pre-established beliefs and values, sociologists argue that a process of .... is occurring.

Democracy

Identify three characteristics of a democracy.

1 ....

2 ....

3 ....

Demystification

Circle the odd one out, giving a reason for your choice.

demystification   disengagement   disenchantment

Denomination

Fill in the blanks, using the words from the list below.

A denomination is a **1** .... religious organisation usually regarded as lying **2** .... between a **3** .... and a **4** .... in terms of its characteristics. Denominations are **5** .... and tend to support the existing **6** .... They have a **7** .... organisational structure and a **8** ...., relatively **9** ...., membership.

formal   mid-way   Christian   sect   social order
stable   church   well established   wide

Dependency theory

Sort out the following statements into strengths or weaknesses of dependency theory.

1 It is a realistic description of the relationships between the First and Third Worlds.

2 It focuses on the historical development of relationships between the First and Third Worlds.

3 It offers an ongoing view of relationships between the First and Third Worlds.

4 It offers a definition of dependency that does not cover all cases of dependency.

5 It ignores the willing acceptance of capitalism by many Third World countries.

6 It is less optimistic of relationships between First and Third Worlds than modernisation theory.

7 It offers a unidimensional view of the nature of dependency.

8 It downplays exploitation of the First World by the Second World.

9 It is an economic determinist theory.

10 It offers a complex view of relationships between the First and Third Worlds through the operation of enclaves.

Deskilling

Match up the following concepts on the left with the definitions on the right, by connecting with arrows.

I Deskilling	The process whereby new technologies strip away traditional skills and introduce new skills to manual and non-manual workers.
2 Reaggregation of tasks	The process whereby occupational roles are divided up into small routine activities, so that divisions between workers are introduced.
3 Reskilling	The process whereby new technologies strip away traditional skills from workers, whether manual or non-manual.
4 Social division of labour	The process whereby production roles are specialised into broad occupations, producing dependency between individuals.
5 Detailed division of labour	The process whereby the splitting of work tasks into small routines is reversed so that workers produce the whole of a product, not just a small part.

Determinism

Distinguish between the Marxist and functionalist views of determinism as the basis of social behaviour.

....

....

....

....

....

Development

Distinguish between the following terms.

1 (a) Developed societies	(b) Undeveloped societies	(c) Underdeveloped societies
....	....	....
....	....	....
....	....	....
....	....	....
....	....	....
2 (a) Evolutionary theory	(b) Teleological theory	(c) Convergence theory
....	....	....
....	....	....
....	....	....
....	....	....
....	....	....
2 (a) Social development	(b) Economic development	(c) Political development
....	....	....
....	....	....
....	....	....
....	....	....
....	....	....
3 (a) Urbanisation	(b) Suburbanisation	(c) Deurbanisation
....	....	....
....	....	....
....	....	....
....	....	....

Deviance

Distinguish between:

Deviance

....

....

Social diversion

....

Social deviations

....

....

Conflict crimes

....

....

Consensus crimes

....

....

Acceptable crimes

....

....

Differential association

For each of the following theories of crime, offer one main feature and one main criticism:

Theory	(a) Feature	(b) Criticism
1 **Differential association**	....	....
2 **Concentric zone**	....	....
3 **Human ecology**	....	....
4 **Urbanism as a way of life**	....	....

Disability

State three criticisms which could be made of the term 'disability'.

1 ....

....

....

2 ....

....

....

3 ....

....

....

Discourse

Decide which of the following statements are true and which are false.

1 The concept of discourse was put forward by Michel Foucault, the French philosopher and sociologist.   True/False

2 A discourse is a number of related statements about things that act to frame the way we can think about those things   True/False

3 A discourse is a statement we believe as true.   True/False

4 Discourses are aspects of power and knowledge.   True/False

5 Individuals can choose the discourses that they employ in everyday life.   True/False

Divorce

Answer the following questions as fully as possible.

1   What is the definition of the divorce rate?

   ....

   ....

2   The divorce rate does not increase steadily from one year to the next, but there are
   sudden peaks, which then level off. Suggest the major reason why these peaks occur.

   ....

   ....

   ....

3   More women now begin petitions for divorce than previously. Suggest one reason why
   this might be.

   ....

   ....

4   Increases in the divorce rate have many explanations. Suggest:

   (a)   one demographical reason for the increases;

   ....

   ....

   (b)   one sociological reason.

   ....

   ....

5   What do sociologists mean by the divorce inheritance?

   ....

   ....

Domestic economy

For each historical period identified, offer a description of the contribution each household member made to the domestic economy.

	(a) Middle 17th century	(b) Early 20th century	(c) Early 21st century
1 Father			
2 Mother			
3 Child			

Domestic labour

Complete the following passage about domestic labour, using the concepts provided.

**capitalism   labour power   childcare   survival   functions
biological   economy   peripheral**

Marxist approaches to domestic labour stress the important role that housework and

1 .... have for the successful operation of 2 .... That is they

argue that domestic labour has vital 3 .... to perform for the capitalist

4 .... In the first place, domestic labour is concerned with the reproduction

of 5 ...., that is the daily refreshment of the worker, so that they are ready to

take a full part in production the following day. Second, it is concerned with the

6 .... reproduction of the labour force, producing the next generation of

labourers to work in capitalist production. Therefore, rather than domestic labour being

seen as a 7 .... and unimportant activity within capitalism, it is central to both

the immediate and long-term 8 .... of capitalism.

Drift

Complete the following passage on the importance of drift in the sociology of crime and deviance, using appropriate sociological terminology.

One of the most important contributions of the 1 .... approach to the

sociology of crime and deviance is the concept of drift. This concept is defined as the way

in which individuals move in and out of criminal activity at various stages of their

2 .... It stands in contrast to the notion of a criminal 3 ...., in

which the criminal is committed to a life of crime and gains 4 ...., power and

income from engaging in it. The emphasis with the notion of drift is on the casual nature

of much crime and deviance and how most people have engaged in it from time to time.

In particular, the young are likely to drift into petty crime, but they go on to

5 .... without obtaining the 6 .... of criminal,

even when they may have been caught and 7 .... as a criminal/deviant.

Dual economy thesis

Complete the following passage, using the concepts found below it.

Reacting against **1** .... theory, Boeke proposed that the operation of the economy in **2** .... countries was not a simple relationship of exploitation. Rather, the activities of **3** .... in the Third World created two separate economies in these countries. The first economy consisted of an **4** .... system, which was linked into the global economy through institutions such as **5** .... and technologies such as **6** .... and cables. This economy was largely unrelated to the second, which consisted of a rural, often **7** .... economy, associated with low levels of technology, **8** .... and limited surpluses. Unlike more **9** .... inspired theories, Boeke argued that these two economies operated relatively independent of one another and did not exist in a chain of **10** ...., which solely benefited the First World.

**Third World   urban-based   Marxist   exploitation
Stock Exchanges   transnational companies   underdevelopment
subsistence   satellites   peasant farming**

Ecumenicalism

Distinguish between the following terms.

1 Ecumenicalism ....
....
....

2 Televangelism ....
....
....

3 Totemism ....
....
....

Educational standards

Write a sentence or two on each of the following concepts or phrases which would contribute to a discussion on the difficulties of measuring 'educational standards'.

1 Pass rates ....

....

....

2 Grammar schools ....

....

....

3 Comprehensivisation ....

....

....

4 Coursework ....

....

....

5 National Curriculum ....

....

....

6 League tables ....

....

....

Embourgeoisement

(A) *Identify three social factors which led to the suggestion that embourgeoisement was taking place in Britain in the 1960s.*

....

....

....

....

....

....

(B) *State three findings from the 'Affluent Worker' study which cast doubt on the embourgeoisement thesis.*

....

....

....

....

....

....

Empowerment

Fill in the missing words, using the list below.

obligations   powerful   New Right   negotiating   right   dispersal   learning

Empowerment is a concept with a varied history and consequently with very different meanings. It has been used by the **1** .... to emphasise the responsibilities and **2** .... of the individual to take control of their own destinies. It has also been used by Liberation theorists to describe the **3** .... of power from the hands of the few to the many. In education, the term is often used in relation to students **4** .... their own educational needs with their teachers and taking responsibility for their own **5** .... The idea has been criticised because it implies that the **6** .... are giving power to the powerless for their own good and ignores the processes where the powerless seek to take power from the powerful as their **7** ....

Equality of opportunity

Identify and explain three factors which may act to prevent equality of opportunity in education.

1 ....

....

....

....

....

2 ....

....

....

....

....

3 ....

....

....

....

....

Ethical issues

The following is a description of the television programme **Big Brother.** *Point out five practices in the programmes that sociologists would not be allowed to perform because they might be thought to be unethical.*

Ten people are isolated from all contact with the real world, except through a single electronic point of contact. They are given orders by a disembodied voice to carry out tasks over a number of weeks. The tasks are related to the amount of food and drink they will have each week, as they gamble with a percentage of their provisions. The ten are under constant and 'hidden' video surveillance in all areas of their living space, including showers and toilets. All conversations are monitored through microphones that all the members have to wear at all times. Each week, every participant nominates two of the others as candidates for eviction. The public then vote out one of two through a telephone and internet poll. The evicted person has only two hours to get ready to leave and then runs a gauntlet of the general public to a studio where s/he is interviewed live about their experiences. There are strict rules about what the participants can and cannot talk about while they are in the environment. The winner is the last person remaining in the environment and they win £70,000.

Ethnicity

Distinguish between the following pairs of concepts, concerned with ethnicity.

1 (a) Ethnicity	**(b)** Race ....
2 (a) Assimilation	**(b)** Hybridisation ....
3 (a) Black	**(b)** Afro-Caribbean ....

Extended family

Match the definitions of these extended family types to the correct concept.

1	Polyandrous family	**(A)**	Where more than two generations live together.
2	Polygamous family	**(B)**	Where one woman takes more than one husband and any consequent children live together.
3	Polygynous family	**(C)**	Where one man takes more than one wife and lives with them and all the children.
4	Horizontally extended family	**(D)**	Where brothers, sisters, their spouses and children live together.
5	Vertically extended family	**(E)**	Where there are more than two people in a sexual relationship and their children.

Family fit

Use the following terms to complete the equations, which describe the theory of fit.

**Pre-industrial society   Democracy   Social mobility   Nuclear family
Agricultural production   Industrial society   Home-based work
Extended family   Factory-based work   Industrial production
Good communications   Patriarchal power   Poor transport
Greater equality   Geographical immobility   Feudal social relations**

Type of society		Characteristics of society		Type of family		Characteristics of family
W	+	A	=	X	+	D
		B				E
		C				F
Y	+	G	=	Z	+	J
		H				K
		I				L

Family size

Identify three reasons why family size in Britain has generally declined over the last 100 years.

1 ....

....

....

2 ....

....

....

3 ....

....

....

Family structure

Match up the family structures, which are features of contemporary family diversity, to the appropriate description, by linking them with arrows.

1 Reconstituted families	**(A)** Where the children of a couple have left home leaving the parents behind. This may be for reasons of education, career or marriage.
2 Empty nest families	**(B)** Where individuals choose to live on their own, whether they have a steady relationship or not. They may have work commitments which enable this arrangement or it may be a life-style choice.
3 Matrifocal families	**(C)** Where lone parent families are headed by the mother, who is the dominant figure in family life. This may be a consequence of divorce, separation or widowhood, or it may be a life-style choice.
4 Singletons	**(D)** Where more than one family come to live together. This may be the consequence of divorce or bereavement.

Feminisation of poverty

State three reasons why women form a disproportionately large group of those in poverty.

1 ....

....

....

2 ....

....

....

3 ....

....

....

Feminisation of work

Though work is seen as increasingly feminised as more and more women go out to work in more and more contexts, it is also accepted that work is segregated by gender. For each of the following explanations of gender differences in work, identify one feature of the explanation, one strength of the explanation and one weakness:

Feature	Strength	Weakness
1 (a) Functionalist theory	(b)	(c) ....
2 (a) Exchange theory	(b)	(c) .... *continued*

3 (a) Conflict theory	(b)	(c)
....	....	....
....	....	....
....	....	....
4 (a) Dual systems theory	(b)	(c)
....	....	....
....	....	....
....	....	....
5 (a) Choice theory	(b)	(c)
....	....	....
....	....	....
....	....	....

Feminism

Identify the feminist perspective from the descriptions given below.

Description	Perspective
1 A belief that women should strive for equal rights with men.	....
2 A view that women are doubly oppressed, by the systems of patriarchy and capitalism.	....
3 A belief that women can coexist with men only if men are prepared to over-throw patriarchy; some believe that this will not happen, and that women can and should exist without men.	....
4 A belief that some women are doubly disadvantaged, by patriarchy and by racism.	....

First world

Distinguish between the following concepts used in world sociology, highlighting any problems of using them.

1 (a) First World	**(b)** Second World	**(c)** Third World ....
2 (a) Undeveloped World	**(b)** Developing World	**(c)** Developed World ....
3 (a) North		**(b)** South ....
4 (a) Information technology	**(b)** Intermediate technology	**(c)** Low-level technology ....
5 (a) Agricultural society	**(b)** Capitalist society	**(c)** Industrial society ....

Five stages of economic growth

Match up the description with each stage of Rostow's schema and with the appropriate example by using arrows.

1 21st century United States	**2** 21st century China	**3** 20th century Nepal	**4** 19th century Germany	**5** 18th century Britain
(A) Traditional society	**(B)** Pre-conditions for take-off	**(C)** Take-off	**(D)** Maturity	**(E)** Developed society
(i) Industry is diverse. Investment as proportion of GNP increases.	**(ii)** Low levels of technology are applied to small-scale agricultural production.	**(iii)** Agriculture is reorganised, so that surplus capital is developed, as is transport.	**(iv)** Visible consumption is the norm with an emphasis on the service economy.	**(v)** Key sectors of the economy are subject to innovatory technologies, exploited by surplus capital.

Folk devils

The following groups have all been cast as 'folk devils' in the popular press and opinion. For each group identify two aspects of their appearance or behaviour that have led to this label being attached to them.

Asylum seekers   **1** ....

                       2 ....

New Age travellers   **1** ....

                       2 ....

Punks   **1** ....

                       2 ....

Yardies   **1** ....

                       2 ....

Formal economy

Distinguish between the following.

1 (a) Formal economy

....

....

....

....

(b) Informal economy

....

....

....

....

2 (a) Black economy

....

....

....

....

(b) Grey economy

....

....

....

....

3 (a) Domestic economy

....

....

....

....

(b) Homeworking

....

....

....

....

4 (a) Communal economy

....

....

....

....

(b) Global economy

....

....

....

....

Functionalism

Give three criticisms of functionalism.

1 ....

....

2 ....

....

3 ....

....

Fundamentalism

Briefly explain what is meant by 'fundamentalism'.

....

....

....

....

....

....

....

....

Gatekeepers

The concept of gatekeeper can be used in several different areas of sociology. It is most commonly used in the study of the mass media, but has also been employed in the sociology of science.

1   Using either the media or science, offer a definition of gatekeeping.

....

....

....

....

....

2   In both cases, what do sociologists believe is the main function of gatekeepers?

Mass media

....

....

Sociology of science

....

....

3   In both cases, identify two social or organisational positions, which can act as gatekeepers.

Mass media

(1) ....

(2) ....

Sociology of science

(1) ....

(2) ....

Gender

For each of the following areas of social life, identify one way in which females are disadvantaged and one way in which the position of females has changed in the last century.

(a) Disadvantage	(b) Change
1 Family	....
2 Education	....
3 Politics	....
4 Work	....
5 Media	....

Gender codes

Distinguish between:

1 **(a)** Gender codes

....

....

....

(b) Gender regime

....

....

....

2 **(a)** Gender

....

....

(b) Sex

....

....

....

3 **(a)** Gender stereotype

....

....

....

(b) Genderquake

....

....

....

Globalisation

Match the concepts on the left-hand side with the appropriate definition on the right, by linking with arrows.

1 Globalisation

2 Localisation

3 Space–time distanciation

4 Imagined community

5 Disembedding process

(A) The process whereby social relations are extracted from local situations and placed on a global footing.

(B) The process whereby groups based on linguistic, regional or ethnic identities are given space within a world context.

(C) The process whereby culture, economics and politics are increasingly situated on a world scale.

(D) The process whereby relationships can be thought of as having a world dimension.

(E) The process whereby events are experienced immediately through the media, regardless of their point of origin.

Golden age of religion

Explain briefly how reference to the 'golden age of religion' could be important to a discussion on secularisation.

....

....

....

....

....

....

....

....

....

....

Green revolution

Complete the following sentences about the green revolution and environmentalism from the endings provided.

1 The main features of the green revolution are

(A) a recognition of the global other and a sensitivity to the environment.

2 The main features of the concept of Gaia are

(B) the inclusion of plants and respect for the animal kingdom.

3 The main features of a global community are

(C) greenhouse gases and chemical contamination.

4 The main features of global pollution are

(D) genetic modification and the use of pesticides.

5 The main features of an imagined community are

(E) a respect for the world as a whole and treating the earth as a subject.

Hawthorne effect

From the following descriptions distinguish between the Hawthorne effect, the halo effect, interviewer bias, prompting and hostility.

1 The respondent reacts to the social characteristics of the researcher in either a positive or negative way.   ....

2 The respondent does not respond fully because they feel intimidated by or uncomfortable with the researcher.   ....

3 Participants act in a different way from usual because they know they are being observed by a researcher.   ....

4 Respondents reply to questions with answers which they think the researcher wants to hear.   ....

5 The manner of the researcher suggests a particular response to the respondent.   ....

Headlining

Complete the following criticisms of the concept of headlining in the newspapers by choosing the appropriate phrase from the list.

1 Editors headline particular stories because they are giving the public ....

2 Readers of headlines do not always read them, because of the ....

3 In choosing to headline a story, editors employ ....

4 Editors are not only influenced by the desire to maximise sales in choosing stories, but also by ....

5 Different newspapers headline similar issues, because it is often obvious ....

what is in the public interest   process of selective exposure

what they want to read about   what the main news items of the day are

news values such as closeness to home

Health

1 Explain the difference between morbidity and mortality.

....

....

2 Explain why it is difficult to measure 'health'.

....

....

....

Health care

1 Explain what is meant by 'the inverse care law'.

....

....

....

2 Give three examples of how health care may be unequally distributed between social groups.

(a) ....

....

(b) ....

....

....

(c) ....

....

....

Hegemony

(a) Briefly explain what is meant by 'hegemony'.

....

....

....

(b) Suggest three ways in which Marxists claim that subordinate groups in society are persuaded to accept the values of the dominant class.

(i) ....

(ii) ....

(iii) ....

Hidden curriculum

Complete the following table by identifying two other things that pupils may learn through the hidden curriculum, explaining for each how this may be achieved.

What may be learned	How this may be learned
(a) Belief that certain subjects are superior to others.	**(b)** The attitudes of teachers and pupils involved in those subjects; restricting access to certain subjects.

69

Home background

Write a few paragraphs showing how pupils' home backgrounds can exert an influence over their educational achievement, making sure that you incorporate all the terms shown below, though not necessarily in that order.

working class   middle class   cultural capital   ethnic minority

parental aspirations   language   deferred gratification

negative stereotypes   knowledge of the education system

....

....

....

....

....

....

....

....

....

....

....

....

....

....

....

....

....

....

....

Household

Distinguish between:

1 **(a)** Household

....
....
....

....

(b) Family

....
....
....

....

2 **(a)** Household economy

....
....
....
....
....

(b) Domestic labour

....
....
....
....
....

3 **(a)** Child-centredness

....
....
....
....
....

(b) Home-centredness

....
....
....
....
....

Human Relations School

Offer a description for each of these concepts or phrases, associated with, or a criticism of, the Human Relations School. Identify whether each is a feature or a criticism.

1 Work as a central life interest

....

....

2 Self-actualisation

....

....

3 Cow sociology

....

....

4 Culture of engagement

....

....

5 Covert techniques of control

....

....

6 Post–Fordism

....

....

7 Flexible specialisation

....

....

8 Neo-Fordism

....

....

9 Relationships of indifference

....

....

10 Dispersal of control

....

....

Hyper-reality

Complete the following sentences, supplying an appropriate sociologist or sociological concept. The first letter is given to you as an aid.

1 The concept of hyper-reality was introduced by B............................ .

2 Hyper-reality is to be found in i............................ found in the mass media

3 Our knowledge of the world is m............................ through the media.

4 Real events in the world are no longer experienced directly, but through r............................ in the media.

5 The concept of hyper-reality has been criticised for m............................ the violence and suffering experienced by real people in world events.

Hypothesis

Match up each concept on the right with the appropriate definition and then rearrange the list into the correct order for the hypothetico–deductive method.

1... Experiment   A verified statement that explains the phenomenon.

2... Hypothesis   Examination of a phenomenon of interest.

3... Observation   A possible statement of explanation of the phenomenon.

4... Theory   Testing explanations.

latrogenesis

Complete the table by stating which of the following statements represents (a) clinical iatrogenesis, (b) social iatrogenesis and (c) cultural iatrogenesis, and give an example of each.

Statement	Form of iatrogenesis	Example
1 The process by which individuals increasingly hand over the power and desire to look after themselves to health professionals.	....	....
2 The power of medical ideology and the increasing medicalisation of physical and mental conditions.	....	....
3 The risks to health from medical treatment itself.	....	....

Identity

Indicate whether the following statements about the sociological concept of identity are true or false.

1 Our identities are fixed at birth.   True/False

2 The concept of identity is associated with the ideas of post-modernity.   True/False

3 Religion and class of origin are two sources of identity.   True/False

4 Identity is solely a matter of individual choice.   True/False

5 We can adopt different identities in different situations.   True/False

Identity construction

Using sexual identity as an example, suggest the ways in which the following factors might influence the construction of an identity.

1 Family

....

....

2 Legislation

....

....

3 Social movements

....

....

4 Economics

....

....

5 Science

....

....

6 Media

....

....

Ideology

Read the statements below and indicate for each one whether it is an example of primarily right-wing or left-wing ideology.

Statement	Right-wing	Left-wing
1 Society is based on the survival of the fittest; those at the top are the strongest and most suited to rule.		
2 There is no such thing as 'society'; there are just individuals.		
3 A good society is based on co-operation, with people helping those less fortunate than themselves.		
4 It is the duty of the state to ensure a decent standard of living for everyone.		
5 The state should intervene as little as possible in people's lives.		
6 Taxation should be as low as possible to provide the wealthy with an incentive to work and create more wealth which will then trickle down to benefit those in the lower social classes.		
7 Taxation should be used as a means of ensuring a more equal distribution of wealth and income in society.		
8 People should take out a private pension to provide for their old age and not rely on the state to look after them.		

Illness

Complete the following sentences by inserting the appropriate concept.

1 The belief that a particular germ causes a particular disease is the doctrine of
....

2 .... refers to the study of the nature, amount and spread of a disease in order to understand its cause(s) and develop an appropriate treatment/cure.

3 The .... of illness sees disease as a temporary phenomenon which will disappear with appropriate treatment.

Income

Circle the odd one out, giving a reason for your choice.

interest on savings   pension payments   £2000 of Premium Bonds

....

....

....

....

Index of deprivation

Fill in the blanks using the words at the end.

This is a way of measuring **1** .... based on a list of **2** ....

considered by most people as things everybody should be able to **3** .... The

index covers **4** .... goods, **5** .... amenities, **6** ....

activities and **7** .... Poverty is defined as a **8** .... of three or more

items on the list. Use of the index of deprivation reveals that millions of people are forced

to live without things a **9** .... of the population consider **10** ....

nutrition   majority   necessities   lack   poverty   social
afford   essential   material   household

Indicators of class

Give three reasons why occupation is often used as the major indicator of class.

1 ....

2 ....

3 ....

Individuation

Complete the following sentences by inserting the appropriate concept.

1 Individuation refers to a process whereby religious bodies and institutions become less important to a person's search for ....

2 Late-modern and post-modern societies are characterised by a proliferation of religious and spiritual organisations and groups, many characterised by the term '...................................
.... '.

3 Many people are rejecting the more traditional forms of religious experience and looking for something which they see as more .... and more suited to their own particular ....

Industrial conflict

Circle the odd one out in each set of three concepts concerned with industrial conflict, giving a reason for your choice.

1 **Grievance procedure;   Industrial sabotage;   Strike**

2 **Official strike;   Union sanctioned work-to-rule;   Mass absenteeism**

3 **Sympathy strike;   Balloted strike;   Union picket of six**

....

....

....

Industrialisation

Suggest five positive and five negative consequences of a society industrialising, which have been suggested by sociologists. Describe each consequence in no more than two sentences.

(a) Positive consequences	(b) Negative consequences
1	1 ....
2	2 ....
3	3 ....
4	4 ....
5	5 ....

Inequality

Complete the following by giving an example of inequality between social classes for each of the three areas mentioned.

Area of inequality	Example
1 Health care	....
2 Education	....
3 Housing	....

Infant mortality rate

Suggest three reasons for the fall in the infant mortality rate over the last century.

1 ....

....

2 ....

....

3 ....

....

Inheritance

Explain what is meant by 'inheritance', and explain how this contributes to the continuation of inequality in society.

....

....

....

....

....

....

Interactionism

Identify the particular type of interactionism from the description.

Description	Type of interactionism
1 Individuals define situations and act according to those definitions. Social life is possible because many of those definitions are shared, and are constructed from the symbols learned and communicated through interaction with others.	....
2 In their interactions with others, people use techniques of impression management to create a particular image of themselves in a particular context.	....
3 People construct their everyday world from the reactions of others; they operate according to a taken-for-granted reality which is rarely questioned.	....
4 The social world is built up of often arbitrary rules arising out of shared background knowledge. Understanding of these processes can only be gained by disrupting or challenging these taken-for-granted realities.	....

Interviews

Distinguish between

1 (a) Formal interviews; **(b)** informal interviews

....
....
....
....

2 (a) Structured interviews; **(b)** semi-structured interviews; **(c)** unstructured interviews

....
....
....
....
....

3 (a) Interview schedule; **(b)** interview transcript

....
....
....
....

4 (a) Standardised interviews; **(b)** in-depth interviews

....
....
....
....
....

Juvenile delinquency

Place the following statements into the appropriate explanation for why young, especially working-class, males tend to commit more crime:

(a) Some young men in working-class areas are socialised into criminal careers.

(b) Young working-class men are more likely to hang around the street with time on their hands.

(c) The values of toughness and machismo set young men against authority.

(d) Young working-class men are more likely not to succeed in education.

(e) Young working-class men are often marginalised from mainstream society.

(f) Young working-class men are more likely to socialise with active criminals and 'learn their trade'.

I Status	2 Opportunity	3 Culture
....	....	....
....	....	....
....	....	....
....	....	....
....	....	....
....	....	....
....	....	....

Labelling theory

Match the definitions on the right-hand side with the concepts on the left.

1 Labelling

    (A) The processes of 'normative deviance' which are committed by most people and accepted or tolerated by others.

2 Primary deviance

    (B) Those who commit deviant acts, but are not seen by others as committing those acts.

3 Falsely accused

    (C) The process whereby individuals or groups have identities attached to them, which constitute a stereotype shorthand for them.

4 Master status

    (D) Those who commit deviant acts and are seen by others as committing those acts.

5 Secondary deviance

    (E) The process whereby a deviant identity becomes the main way in which an individual or group is perceived by others.

6 True deviants

    (F) Those who do not commit deviant acts, but are seen by others as doing so.

7 Secret deviants

    (G) The process whereby the successful application of a deviant identity to an individual or group leads to subsequent actions being seen by others in terms of that identity.

Language codes

For each of the following statements, say whether it is true or false.

Statement	True/False
1 Work on language codes is primarily associated with the sociologist Basil Bernstein.	....
2 Language codes are taught in school.	....
3 Working class children talk in restricted code and middle-class children talk in elaborated code.	....
4 The elaborated code is characterised by grammatically complex structures.	....
5 Restricted code is often used when the conversation refers to a shared context in which much of the meaning is implicit.	....
6 Most teaching takes place using the restricted code.	....
7 Labov has criticised much of the work on language codes, arguing that the research failed to recognise the richness and complexity of working-class speech.	....
8 While the original work on language codes focused on class-based forms of speech, the arguments could also be applied to the speech patterns of some ethnic minority groups.	....

Legitimation

For each of the following, briefly explain the basis of that person's claim to legitimacy with respect to power.

1 A medieval king ....

....

2 The Prime Minister ....

....

3 A police officer ....

....

4 The Pope ....

....

5 The Queen ....

....

Leisure

Offer a definition for the following approaches to the sociology of leisure. For each approach, suggest two criticisms of the approach.

1 Compensatory approach	....	(a) ....
	....	
	....	
	....	(b) ....
	....	
	....	
	....	
2 Segmentalist approach	....	(a) ....
	....	
	....	
	....	(b) ....
	....	
	....	
	....	
3 Holist approach	....	(a) ....
	....	
	....	
	....	(b) ....
	....	
	....	
	....	

Liberation theology

Complete the following by identifying the correct definition of liberation theology, and stating which concepts are described by the remaining two definitions.

Definition	Concept
1 A Weberian concept referring to religious explanations which provide a justification for social inequalities, and which state that those suffering from such inequalities would be rewarded in the afterlife.	....
2 A belief that people have a duty to try to free themselves from forms of oppression in this life, rather than waiting for earthly wrongs to be put right in the next world.	....
3 A society ruled by members of a religious group, such as a priest caste, who control the population by their privileged access to religious rituals and meanings.	....

Life chances

Write a sentence on each of the following to contribute to a discussion on differential life chances by social class.

1 Standardised mortality ratio ....

....

....

....

2 Education ....

....

....

....

continued

3   The post-code distribution of health care ....

....

....

....

4   Type of occupation ....

....

....

....

5   Housing tenure ....

....

....

....

Logic of industrialism

Distinguish between:

1   **(a)** logic of industrialism thesis   **(b)** post-industrial society theory

....

....

....

2   **(a)** one-way convergence   **(b)** two-way convergence

....

....

....

3   **(a)** end of ideology theory   **(b)** three roads to modernity

....

....

....

Lone-parent families

Complete the following paragraph about lone-parent families, using your sociological knowledge of their situation.

Also called one-parent or **1** .... families, there has been a noticeable rise in the proportion of children who are brought up in lone-parent families. More often than not, the parent is the **2** .... rather than the **3** .... While the stereotype of lone parents presented in the media is of the wilful, often teenage woman, getting pregnant to jump the **4** ...., the reality is very different. Lone parent situations are caused by more than one factor. The death of a spouse or the **5** .... of the parents are also reasons why lone-parent families come about. Nor should it be imagined that lone-parent families are without any support. As well as receiving benefits from the **6** ...., many lone parents have wider networks of family and **7** .... who can be called upon to assist in the bringing-up of the children. Nevertheless, children of lone parents are a significant sector of the **8** ...., especially where the children are of pre-school age and likely to make it difficult for the lone parent to gain well-paid work. The lack of affordable and reliable **9** .... facilities in many areas also militates against lone parents gaining employment.

Loss of family functions

Parsons argued that the family increasingly loses functions to outside bureaucracies as a society industrialises, leaving it only with core activities to perform. This allows the family to specialise in what it does best. Give three criticisms of this point of view.

1 ....

....

2 ....

....

3 ....

....

Marriage

For each of the following concepts, write a couple of sentences which would contribute to a discussion of whether marriage is in decline in modern society.

1 Remarriage

....

....

....

....

2 Serial monogamy

....

....

....

....

3 Step families

....

....

....

....

4 Illegitimacy

....

....

....

....

5 Delayed motherhood

....

....

....

....

Marxism

Write a brief definition of each of the following concepts, all associated with Marxism.

1 Dialectic

....

....

....

2 Ruling class ideology

....

....

....

3 Ideological state apparatus

....

....

....

4 Substructure (or base)

....

....

....

5 Historical materialism

....

....

....

Mass culture

Complete the following passage, using the words or phrases listed below.

mass society   freedom   inferior   authentic

high tastes   negative   golden age   trivial

low living standards

There are pessimistic and optimistic views of mass culture. Pessimistic views tend

to emphasise a **1** .... of the past, which has somehow been lost as

2 .... has developed. In this view, mass culture is seen as an

3 .... form of culture, debasing the high ideals or **4** ....

cultures of the past. Mass culture is therefore seen in negative terms, with

adjectives such as 'apathetic', **5** ...., 'junk' or 'plastic' being applied to

it. Optimistic views, however, see the past in **6** .... terms,

emphasising the poverty of culture associated with **7** .... In this

approach, mass culture is seen as offering greater choice to individuals, and as

opening up the **8** .... of the elite to all members of society. Mass

culture is therefore described in positive terms, such as enlightenment,

empowerment, **9** .... and choice.

Mass media

Place the following list of mass media technologies in chronological order, starting with the earliest. For each of these technologies identify a specific feature which distinguishes it from previous mass media inventions.

television   megaphone   radio   telegraph   digital television
satellite communications   Internet

Chronological order	Specific features
1	....
2	....
3	....
4	....
5	....
6	....
7	....

Mass society

Some sociologists have argued that modern societies are becoming mass societies as they lose their traditional characteristics. For each of the following features of a mass society, suggest one way in which it has been criticised by sociologists.

1 In a mass society, individuals are atomised into an amorphous (without shape) anomic (without norms) body.

....

....

....

2 In a mass society, intermediate groups such as the family decline in importance.

....

....

....

3 In a mass society, the media offer 'dumbed down' entertainment that enslaves rather than enlightens people.

....

....

....

4 In a mass society, the state becomes very powerful and threatens the liberty of individual citizens.

....

....

....

5 In a mass society, people are told what to think by a media dominated by corporate interests.

....

....

....

Media effects

Link the correct theory of media effects (on the left) to the appropriate description on the right-hand side of the page.

1 Uses and gratifications

2 Two-step model

3 Hypodermic syringe approach

4 Ideological hegemony approach

5 Empty bucket theory

(A) The effect of the media is to transmit ruling-class ideas into the minds of subordinate groups in society.

(B) The effect of the media is to fill up the audience with whatever messages the producers want.

(C) The effects of the media are direct in individuals' lives, as they passively accept the messages contained within it.

(D) The effect of the media is mediated through intervening factors such as opinion leaders.

(E) The effect of the media depends upon what individuals want to gain from them.

Media industries

Fill in the missing blanks from the list below.

The concept of media industries emphasises the **1** .... importance of the mass media in **2** .... societies, rather than just the **3** .... dimension that sociologists have traditionally been concerned with. This focus looks at the centrality of the media in **4** ...., to the extent that they are more profitable than **5** .... industry in First World economies. The dominance of media industries can be seen in the phenomenal growth of information and communications technologies such as the **6** ...., which has seen the share price of **7** .... companies rise sharply, even where they have as yet made little profit. As **8** .... technology becomes common, the media industries will become increasingly inter-related, so that, for example, Internet access will be possible through your **9** .... Interactivity will also become the norm as higher **10** .... connections to domestic houses become commonplace.

**postmodern   manufacturing   bandwidth   'dot.com'   cultural   Internet
television   wealth creation   economic   digital**

Media representations

For each of the following social groups, suggest one stereotype in which the media represents them in a negative light and suggest a way in which the group can be represented positively.

(a) Negative representation	(b) Positive representation
1 Lone mothers	
2 Homosexuals	
3 New Age travellers	
4 Women	
5 Afro-Caribbeans	

Mediation

For each of the following statements about mediation as used by sociologists of the mass media, state whether it is true or false.

1 Mediation is the process whereby the meaning of an individual's experiences is changed into something else.

True/False

2 Mediation is the process whereby ruling-class ideology appears in a disguised form in media content.

True/False

3 Mediation is about negotiations between the owners of media organisations and their employees.

True/False

4 Mediation is about the operation of the middle level of management in media organisations.

True/False

5 News values are the means by which mediation occurs in the presentation of events.

True/False

Medical model

Complete the paragraph below by inserting the appropriate word from the list below.

The medical model of health and illness is also known as the **1** .... model. It is geared towards the **2** .... rather than the **3** .... of illness or disease. There is an emphasis on the **4** .... appearances, or **5** ...., of disease, and little attention is paid to the patient's **6** .... identity. The link between physical and **7** .... well-being, and the importance of the social **8** .... of the patient, tends to be ignored. Disease is seen as something which threatens an individual in a temporary, or **9** ...., fashion. There is also the belief that the best place for treatment is in a **10** .... environment rather than the place where the symptoms arose.

mental symptoms episodic prevention medical environment
organic biomechanical cure social

Medical technology

Identify and briefly explain two criticisms of the view that the increased use of medical technology has helped to bring about better health.

1 ....
....
....
....

2 ....
....
....
....

Medicalisation

Write a brief paragraph on the increasing medicalisation of society, making reference to each of the following.

reproduction   childbirth   sadness   stress   sexuality

....
....
....
....
....
....
....
....
....
....

Mental illness

Identify the missing concepts from the sentences below, then rearrange the first letter of each of them to form a word often used in the discussion of mental illness.

1 There is no clear-cut .... of mental illness.

2 Trowler has shown that mental illness is .... distributed.

3 .... are the gender group most likely to commit suicide.

4 Deviation from .... is often seen as a sign of mental illness.

5 .... is a controversial form of treatment used on some people defined as mentally ill.

6 .... suggested that the label 'mental illness' was a form of social control which enabled the locking-up of some people who did not conform.

7 '...............................' behaviour is often viewed as one of the first signs of mental illness.

Meta-narrative

Explain what is meant by 'meta-narrative'.

....

....

....

....

Metropolis

Offer a definition of the following concepts associated with dependency theory.

1 Metropolis ....

....

....

....

2 Satellite ....

....

....

....

3 Enclave ....

....

....

....

4 Settled colonialism ....

....

....

....

5 Post-colonialism ....

....

....

....

Middle class

For each of the following factors, show how differences exist within middle-class groups.

1 Occupation ....
....
....
....

2 Status ....
....
....
....

3 Life-style ....
....
....
....

4 Housing tenure ....
....
....
....

5 Skills ....
....
....
....

Modernisation theory

Modernisation theory offers the following as explanations for poverty in Third World countries. Expand each of the explanations to show how the factor would affect development prospects and offer one criticism of each.

1 Too many people	2 Too few entrepreneurs	3 Too little capital
(a) Expansion		
....	....	....
....	....	....
....	....	....
....	....	....
....	....	....
....	....	....
....	....	....
(b) Criticism		
....	....	....
....	....	....
....	....	....
....	....	....
....	....	....
....	....	....

Modernity

Complete the following by briefly describing the main characteristics of modernity in each of the spheres shown.

Sphere	Characteristics
1 Political	....
2 Economic	....
3 Social stratification	....
4 Religious	....
5 Scientific	....

Mortality rate

Explain the difference between life expectancy and the mortality rate.

....

....

....

....

....

....

National Curriculum

State three reasons in favour of, and three against, schools having to adopt a National Curriculum.

Reasons in favour

1 ....

....

....

2 ....

....

....

3 ....

....

....

Reasons against

4 ....

....

....

5 ....

....

....

6 ....

....

....

National Health Service

Make brief notes on each of the following as a contribution to a debate on the National Health Service.

1   The 'welfare principle'

....

....

....

....

2   Abolition of the means test

....

....

....

....

3   The Black Report

....

....

....

....

4   Demographic changes in society

....

....

....

....

5   Private health care

....

....

....

....

continued

6 'Care in the community'

....
....
....
....

7 The 'internal market'

....
....
....
....

8 The growth of consumerism

....
....
....
....

9 The Acheson Report 1998

....
....
....
....

10 Bureaucratisation

....
....
....
....

New Christian Right

State whether the following statements about the New Christian Right are true or false.

1   The New Christian Right is a single, organised religious group.   ....

2   The New Christian Right is found only in the United States.   ....

3   Members of the New Christian Right support what they see as 'traditional family values'.   ....

4   In the United States, the New Christian Right is able to influence policy making, as in some states, it represents a considerable proportion of voters.   ....

5   There is no evidence that British political parties are influenced in their policy-making by the views of the New Christian Right.   ....

New deviancy theory

Sort the following statements about new deviancy theory in terms of whether they represent (a) its reaction against earlier theories, (b) what it proposes itself or (c) a criticism of it. Label each statement either R(eaction), P(roposition) or C(riticisms).

1   There is a romantic view of people.   ....

2   Everyone is potentially deviant.   ....

3   There are no criminal subcultures.   ....

4   The working class are not more criminal.   ....

5   There are no criminal types.   ....

6   Society is not totally brutalising.   ....

7   The working class have less power to resist the powerful's labels.   ....

8   People on the margins of society are expressive deviants, resisting capitalism.   ....

9   The concentration on deviance masks more serious and violent criminal activity.   ....

New religious movements

State five characteristics of 'new religious movements'.

1 ....
....

2 ....
....

3 ....
....

4 ....
....

5 ....
....

New social movements

Circle the odd one out, giving reasons for your answer.

The Masonic movement   **Greenpeace**   **The Countryside Alliance**

....
....
....
....
....
....

New vocationalism

(A) *State briefly what is meant by the 'new vocationalism' in education.*

....

....

(B) *For each of the programmes or skills below, say whether it represents part of the new vocationalism, explaining why or why not.*

Programme/Skill	Yes/No	Explanation
1 GCSE maths	....	....
2 Youth Training Schemes	....	....
3 The ability to read and write	....	....
4 IT skills	....	....
5 GNVQ courses	....	....

Newly industrialising countries (NICs)

What do the following sets of countries have in common, which might help to categorise them as newly industrialising countries? For each set, put forward a different factor.

1 Saudi Arabia   Kuwait   Bahrain

....

....

2 Hong Kong   Singapore

....

....

3 Brazil   Malaysia   South Korea

....

....

4 Poland   Czech Republic   Hungary

....

....

News values

The following made-up article in a newspaper demonstrates many of the news values which would make the story attractive to an editor. Audit the story, drawing arrows from elements of the story and writing down what news value is being illustrated. An example is given to start you off.

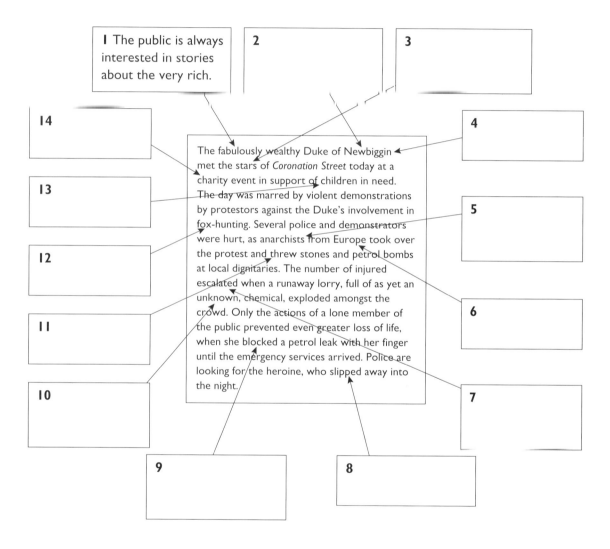

1 The public is always interested in stories about the very rich.

2

3

14

13

12

11

10

4

5

6

7

9

8

The fabulously wealthy Duke of Newbiggin met the stars of *Coronation Street* today at a charity event in support of children in need. The day was marred by violent demonstrations by protestors against the Duke's involvement in fox-hunting. Several police and demonstrators were hurt, as anarchists from Europe took over the protest and threw stones and petrol bombs at local dignitaries. The number of injured escalated when a runaway lorry, full of as yet an unknown, chemical, exploded amongst the crowd. Only the actions of a lone member of the public prevented even greater loss of life, when she blocked a petrol leak with her finger until the emergency services arrived. Police are looking for the heroine, who slipped away into the night.

Norms

Distinguish between:

1 **(a)** Norms

....
....
....
....

(b) Values

....
....
....
....

2 **(a)** Normative order

....
....
....
....

(b) Normative power

....
....
....
....

3 **(a)** Normlessness

....
....
....
....

(b) Normative reference

....
....
....
....

4 **(a)** Normal science

....
....
....
....

(b) Normalising judgements

....
....
....
....

North–South

Place the following countries, where possible, into North or South categories, depending on their stage of development.

**Great Britain   Kenya   Singapore   Australia   Colombia   South Korea   Poland
Malaysia   South Africa   India   Argentina   Malta   Japan   Taiwan**

North   South

....
....
....

Give reasons why some of these countries were difficult to place.

....
....
....

Write a paragraph on the implications of this difficulty for the North–South distinction.

....
....
....

Nuclear family

Answer the following questions about the nuclear family.

1   Which sociological perspective sees the nuclear family
    as best suited to the needs of an industrial society?   ....

2   Name one social scientist who saw the nuclear
    family as 'a source of all our ills'.   ....

3   Which sociological perspective sees the nuclear
    family as essential for the maintenance of capitalism?   ....

4   Which sociological perspective sees the family as a
    patriarchal form?   ....

5   Which perspective sees the nuclear family as the
    moral foundation of society?   ....

Observation

Distinguish between:

1 **(a)** Participant observation; **(b)** Non-participant observation

....

....

....

....

2 **(a)** Unobtrusive observation; **(b)** Obtrusive observation

....

....

....

....

3 **(a)** Covert participant observation; **(b)** Semi-covert participant observation;
   (c) Overt participant observation

....

....

....

....

4 **(a)** Laboratory observation; **(b)** Field observation

....

....

....

....

Occupational structure

Below is a table showing the new socio–economic classification of the occupational structure, used in the 2001 National Census. Occupations are now classified according to the employment contract, including working conditions, prospects and job security. At the bottom is a list of the percentages of the working population employed in each group. Put the appropriate figure alongside each group.

Group	Examples	% of working population
1 Higher managerial and professional	Employers of more than 25 staff, senior managers, doctors, dentists, lawyers	....
2 Lower managerial and professional	Junior managers, police sergeants, teachers, social workers, journalists	....
3 Intermediate	Police constables, firefighters, junior prison officers	....
4 Small employers and own-account workers	Non-professionals who employ fewer than 25 staff	....
5 Lower supervisory and technical	Foremen, supervisors, train drivers	....
6 Semi-routine	Shop assistants, call centre workers	....
7 Routine	Drivers, cleaners	....

Percentages: **23.5   18.6   14.0   12.7   11.0   9.9   9.8**

Official statistics

Place the following types of secondary data into the appropriate category.

**diaries   crime figures   birth registrations   death registrations
newspaper articles   Hansard accounts   suicide rates   autobiographies
incidence of strikes   census data   letters   government reports**

1 Hard official statistics	(A) ....
	(B) ....
	(C) ....
2 Soft official statistics	(A) ....
	(B) ....
	(C) ....
3 Personal documents	(A) ....
	(B) ....
	(C) ....
4 Public documents	(A) ....
	(B) ....
	(C) ....

Operational control

Offer a definition for each of these features of operational control.

1 Span of control

....

....

....

....

2 Hiring and firing

....

....

....

....

3 Secondary power

....

....

....

....

4 Performance-related pay

....

....

....

....

5 'The buck stops here'

....

....

....

....

Opinion leaders

Complete the following flow chart with appropriate information from the choices below.

**Selective interpretation in a social context   Encoding process
Seen as experts in their field   Interpret national news sources
Intentions of media personnel   Standing between media and audience
Ideological content   Representation of social groups
Focus on domestic news   Decoding process   Interpret regional
news sources   Focus on international news**

Producers of media messages

1 ....

2 ....

↓

Media messages

3 ....

4 ....

↓

Opinion leaders

5 ....

6 ....

Local opinion leaders	Cosmopolitan opinion leaders
7	9 ....
8	10 ....

Audience for media messages

11 ....

12 ....

Other

State which is the odd one out in these groups of three, related to the concept of Other, giving your reason for your choices.

1 Whites   Gays   Males

2 Stigmatisation   Marginalisation   Incorporation

3 Roman Catholic   Church of England   Presbyterian

Parental attitudes to education

Suggest three ways in which parental attitudes can affect a child's educational achievement.

1 ....

   ....

   ....

2 ....

   ....

   ....

3 ....

   ....

   ....

Patriarchy

Identify and explain five effects of patriarchy on family life.

	(a) Effect	(b) Explanation
1	....	....
2	....	....
3	....	....
4	....	....
5	....	....

Persistence theories

Briefly explain why persistence theorists would argue that evidence of increased social mobility does not mean that the class structure of Britain has changed.

....

....

....

....

....

Perspectives

State the perspective you would associate with the following groups of concepts.

1 value consensus   biological analogy   social solidarity   ....

2 ideology   alienation   exploitation   ....

3 patriarchal   dual role   gendered   ....

4 ideal type   verstehen   social action   ....

5 meta-narrative   hyper-reality   relativism   ....

Pluralism

Identify and briefly explain three criticisms of the pluralist view of power in society.

1 ....

....

2 ....

....

3 ....

....

Political culture

Match the following descriptions to a particular kind of political culture.

1 A belief that just a few people should govern society.   ....

2 A belief that everyone in a society should have a say in how that society is governed.   ....

3 A belief that there should be a single leader with a set of principles and rules which everyone should follow and where people are punished if they fail to conform.   ....

Political identification

Write a brief paragraph using the words below to contribute to a discussion on dealignment in British politics.

alignment   dealignment   Labour Party   Conservative Party
manual workers   non-manual workers   deviant voters
instrumental   embourgeoisement   volatility   social class
middle-class attitudes and values

....

....

....

....

....

....

....

....

....

....

....

Political participation

Suggest five ways in which people can actively participate in the political process.

1 ....

2 ....

3 ....

4 ....

5 ....

Political party

List three characteristics of a political party.

1 ....

2 ....

3 ....

Politics

Complete the following sentences.

1 Politics is concerned with ....

2 Politics also refers to the workings of the ....

3 Politics is also concerned with national and local ....

Positivism

Give three characteristics of scientific research which positivists believe should be applied to sociological research.

1 ....

2 ....

3 ....

Postmodernity

Offer a definition of the following concepts associated with postmodernity.

1 meta-narrative ....

....

2 society of signs ....

....

3 simulacrum ....

....

4 difference ....

....

5 global culture ....

....

Poverty line

1 *State what is meant by a 'poverty line'.*

....

....

2 *Give three criticisms of the notion of a poverty line.*

(a)...

....

....

(b)...

....

....

(c)...

....

....

Power

Fill in the missing words, using the list of words at the end.

Power refers to the ability of a person or **1** .... to achieve their **2** .... even against the **3** .... of others. Sociologists differ in their **4** .... of who holds power in modern, supposedly . **5** .... societies. **6** .... theorists believe that power is held by a single **7** .... group, while **8** .... argue that power is shared among different **9** .... groups, who seek to influence those who make the important **10** ....

elite   interest   opposition   democratic   group   decisions   pluralists explanation   aims   unified

Practical constraints

Consider the following sentences from a sociological study. For each, identify whether it primarily describes a practical, theoretical or ethical constraint on the research.

1   We decided to adopt a quantitative methodology to provide reliable data.   ....

2   The sample was contained within a limited geographical area to save on travel costs.   ....

3   The research had to be finished before the sample left school in June.   ....

4   We choose to study this issue because of our interest in the nature of social conflict.   ....

5   We decided we had to tell our respondents the real purpose of our research.   ....

6   In a postmodern society, we are suspicious of all meta-narratives.   ....

7   Snowball sampling was the best way of reaching sufficient targets.   ....

8   We did not feel we could personally become involved in that type of activity.   ....

9   Our commitment to the underdog guided us towards particular solutions to the problem.   ....

10   We would have liked to pursue this further, but our report was due in.   ....

125

Pressure groups

State whether each of the following pressure groups is protective or promotional.

1 Friends of the Earth   ....

2 The Child Poverty Action Group   ....

3 National Farmers' Union   ....

4 The Automobile Association   ....

5 The Countryside Alliance   ....

Prestige

Give three criticisms of the use of questionnaires to identify the relative prestige of different occupations.

1 ....
....
....

2 ....
....
....

3 ....
....
....

Primary data

Fill in the missing phrases from the list given below.

Primary data is information that is collected **1** .... It is distinct from secondary data, **2** .... There are a number of different methods used to collect primary data, but the main division is between **3** .... In the case of the former, the most common methods used are **4** .... In the case of the latter, **5** .... are employed. The advantage of primary data over secondary is precisely that it has been collected using **6** .... This ensures that the data is focused on what interests the sociologist and that the design of the research is geared towards collecting the relevant information. Secondary data is collected by others for different purposes, using different categories and methods **7** ....

methods decided by the sociologist
which is material that already exists
structured interviews and questionnaires
which perhaps sociologists would not choose for themselves
primary quantitative data and primary qualitative data
unstructured interviews and various observation techniques
by sociologists themselves

Primary health care

1   *Define what is meant by 'primary health care'.*

    ....

    ....

2   *List three advantages of primary health care.*

    ....

    ....

    ....

Private medicine

Give two arguments in favour, and two against, private medicine and health care.

(a) Arguments in favour	(b) Arguments against
1	1 ....
2	2 ....

Problem of consciousness

Fill in the missing words to show why Marx believed that workers under capitalism would not necessarily have a revolutionary outlook.

1 Workers are subjected to ruling class .... and thus are not always aware of the nature of their ....

2 The most able members of the working class and therefore those most likely to be dissatisfied with their condition may achieve upward ....

3 The ruling class are sometimes forced to make .... to the workers, which defuses revolutionary tendencies.

4 Not all workers experience the same degree of .... deprivation.

Problem of order

Fill in the missing concepts in the passage from the list.

peace solutions optimistic co-operation values
rational calculation selfish coercion

If basic human nature is **1** .... , that is each individual is only concerned with satisfying their own needs, how is it possible that we can live together in relative **2** .... , giving up some of our own desires to establish a society based on order? The **3** .... to this problem of order that have been put forward can be summarised in the following table.

	Positive utilitarianism	**Negative utilitarianism**	**4**	**Consensus**
Description	We agree to give up some of what we want because we all gain so much more by **6** .... rather than conflict.	We agree to give up some of what we want because the consequence of not doing so is the war of all against all, in which life would be uncertain.	We are forced to give up some of what we want because those with power take the lion's share and keep the rest in check by fear of punishment.	We see the importance of giving up some of what we want because agreed **5** .... allow the establishment of fair laws that regulate the behaviour of individuals to the benefit of all.
Basis of order	Rational calculation	**7**	Force	Values/Law
Perspective	**8** .... interactionists	Pessimistic interactionists	Marxists	Functionalists

Profane

1 *Explain what Durkheim meant by 'profane'.*

   ....

   ....

2 *State two criticisms which could be made of the concept.*

   ....

   ....

   ....

Proletarianisation

Give two arguments in favour, and two against, the proposition that the proletarianisation of the workforce is taking place.

Arguments in favour	Arguments against
1	1 ....
2	2 ....

Protestant ethic thesis

Complete the following sentences by inserting the appropriate concept or sociologist.

1   The concept is associated with the sociologist ....

2   The Protestant ethic refers to a set of religious beliefs associated with a 17th-century sect called ....

3   This sect believed that from the moment of creation, God had chosen those who would be 'saved'. This is known as ....

4   Members also believed that 'work' was similar to a religious vocation, or ....

5   Work was thus seen as a way of honouring God, and worldly success came to be seen as a way of indicating that a person was one of the ....

6   The sect emphasised the need for a sober, thrifty life-style, and members did not use their accumulating wealth in displays of ....

7   Rather than spend their profits, sect members used them for ....

8   Weber argued that these particular beliefs, and the consequences which stemmed from them, provided the right social and economic climate for the development of ....

9   Weber thus argued that religious beliefs could therefore be instrumental in bringing about ....

10 In this, he disagreed with Marx, who viewed religion as essentially a .... force.

Qualitative data

Indicate whether you think the following statements about qualitative data are true or false.

1 Official statistics are a form of qualitative data. ....

2 Observational studies usually result in qualitative data. ....

3 Qualitative data are easier to code for a computer than quantitative data. ....

4 Positivists are more likely to favour qualitative data. ....

5 Qualitative data provide rich detailed descriptions of social life. ....

Quantum theory of religion

1 *Explain how the growth in 'New Age' beliefs and practices could be used as evidence to support the quantum theory of religion.*

....

....

....

....

2 *Give a criticism of the concept of the quantum theory of religion.*

....

....

....

Questionnaires

Criticise the following questionnaire, identifying specifically what is wrong with each question.

I What age are you? (please circle)	15–20 21–29 31–39 40–50 60 or over
2 Are you aware of what AIDS is? (please circle)	Yes/No
3 Do you think that AIDS is the result of divine retribution? (please answer fully)	
4 Do you think you can get AIDS from unprotected sex and kissing?	Yes/No
5 What are the effects of AIDS on the immune system? (answer in as much detail as possible)	
6 Would you agree that concerns about AIDS are a moral panic that has been socially constructed?	Yes/No

Realignment theories

1 Explain what is meant by 'realignment theories'.

....

....

....

2 Suggest five divisions, other than social class, into which voters now might fall.

....

....

Relative poverty

With reference to the concepts listed below, briefly explain why the research of sociologists such as Townsend and Mack and Lansley is important to a study of poverty in Britain.

poverty line   relative poverty   normal   desirable

index of deprivation   consensual view of need

....

....

....

....

....

....

....

....

Reliability

Which of the three following definitions is the correct one for reliability. For each of the other two suggest a concept for which it is the definition.

1 The outcome of sociological research correctly
represents the phenomenon it is seeking to describe.   ....

2 The outcome of sociological research can be
applied to similar phenomena in society.   ....

3 The outcome of sociological research would be
identical if the data collection was repeated.   ....

Religion

Distinguish between religion, magic and spiritualism.

....

....

....

....

....

....

....

....

....

Religiosity

Complete the following by showing the difference between the functionalist and the Marxist view of religiosity.

1 **Functionalist view of religiosity**

....

....

....

2 **Marxist view of religiosity**

....

....

....

Religious observance

Distinguish between religious belief and religious observance.

....

....

....

....

....

....

....

....

Reproductive technologies

The increasing use of reproductive technologies to help couples have children raises a number of issues. Give examples below for each of the types of issue raised.

1   Moral/ethical issues

   ....

   ....

   ....

   ....

2   Medical issues

   ....

   ....

   ....

   ....

3   Political issues

   ....

   ....

   ....

   ....

Response rate

Calculate the response rates from each of the following data. Which of the two scenarios would allow generalisation?

Scenario 1.   800 questionnaires sent out, 440 completed and returned.   ....

Scenario 2.   80 questionnaires sent out, 60 completed and returned.   ....

   ....

   ....

   ....

   ....

Ruling class

Complete the following sentences by inserting the appropriate term.

1 The concept of the ruling class is associated with the .... perspective.

2 According to this view, the basis of power of the ruling class is their ownership of
....

3 As well as .... power, the ruling class controls the dominant
.... in society.

4 Even in a society with a democratically elected government, the ruling class will
.... even though it does not ....

5 Some critics of the concept argue that it is not supported by .... evidence.

Sacred

Durkheim suggested that the 'sacred' referred to things 'set apart' and 'forbidden'. Explain why this is not always a satisfactory definition of 'religious' things.

....

....

....

....

....

Sampling

Match the type of sampling procedure on the left with the descriptions on the right, by drawing an arrow between them.

Type of sampling	Description
1 Random sampling	**(A)** Respondents are chosen from predefined social groups proportionately.
2 Quota sampling	**(B)** Every member of the sample has an equal chance of being chosen.
3 Stratified sampling	**(C)** Respondents are chosen according to their conformity to preset criteria.
4 Snowball sampling	**(D)** A respondent suggests further respondents to the sociologist.

Scientific management

(A) *Fill in the missing words in the paragraph, from the following list.*

**natural science   targets   bonuses   experiments   control   profits
incentive   logical   piece work   optimum**

F.W. Taylor produced a system for the **1** .... of workers called scientific management. He argued that the principles of **2** .... could be applied successfully to work, in order to maximise production and thus increase **3** .... By studying the actions of workers through time-and-motion **4** .... , Taylor was able to break down the routines of production into **5** .... parts and establish the **6** .... time for their completion. This allowed managements to set **7** .... for workers, so that maximum effort could be extracted from them. The **8** .... for the worker was contained in **9** .... provisions, where exceeding management's targets for production would result in **10** ....

continued

(B) *Read the following account of events in* **Coronation Street** *in 2000.*

Mike Baldwin's clothing factory in Coronation Street has introduced a piece work system. Janice Battersby and her co-workers signed the new contracts for this system, because it offered the opportunity to make extra wages, once targets had been met. However, the workers have yet to see much extra income. Because the targets have been set at a high level, the women in the factory have to work over lunch-times and after normal hours to even meet their targets, and management has the final say as to which garments count towards the target, because of their powers of quality control. Most of the workers are therefore working hard just to receive the wages they used to get under the old system.

From this account extract two criticisms of scientific management.

1 ....
....

2 ....
....

Secondary data

Circle the odd one out in each of these sets of secondary data. Write a sentence justifying your choice in each case.

1 true romances   movies   news articles   novels

....

2 death statistics   suicide statistics   crime statistics   church attendance statistics

....

3 life histories   diaries   biographies   letters

....

4 government reports   company reports   legislation   orders-in-council

....

Secondary socialisation

Match the aspect of secondary socialisation carried out by schools with the appropriate description on the right using arrows.

Aspects of secondary socialisation	Ways in which this might be carried out in schools
I Respect for authority.	**(A)** The whole class being 'kept in' when one pupil is disobedient.
2 Working as part of a team.	**(B)** Studying a modern foreign language.
3 Learning specialist skills.	**(C)** Having to speak politely to teachers.
4 The application of universalistic principles.	**(D)** Learning subjects such as history and RE.
5 Acquiring knowledge of culturally significant events and beliefs.	**(E)** Being given group tasks to complete.

Sect

Wallis developed a typology of sects depending on whether they were world-rejecting, world-affirming or world-accommodating. Place the following into the appropriate box in the table.

Scientology   The People's Temple   The Manson Family

Neo-pentecostalists   TM

I World-rejecting	2 World-affirming	3 World-accommodating
....	....	....
....	....	....

Secularisation

1   *Explain what is meant by 'secularisation'.*

   ....
   ....
   ....

2   *Give two examples of evidence which could be used in* support *of the secularisation thesis.*

   ....
   ....
   ....
   ....
   ....
   ....

3   *Give two examples of evidence which could be used* against *the secularisation thesis.*

   ....
   ....
   ....
   ....
   ....
   ....

Selective exposure

Offer a definition for these three related processes, using the following concepts correctly. You may use the concepts more than once.

media messages   pre-existing beliefs   Weltanschauung   cognitive
dissonance   choice   intentions of producers   traditional viewing patterns
media content

Selective exposure	Selective interpretation	Selective retention

Self

Distinguish between the following.

1 **(a)** Self .... **(b)** Generalised Other ....

2 **(a)** Looking-glass self .... **(b)** Reflexivity ....

Self-fulfilling prophecy

Identify which of the following scenarios are self-fulfilling prophecies and which are not. For those which are not suggest an alternative label.

Scenario 1

An 11-year-old boy is caught shop-lifting cigarettes, and is arrested by the police. He is too young to be prosecuted, but is given a caution and a serious lecture by a senior police officer. He is warned of the consequences of further offences. He is so shaken by the picture of a dismal future, that he resolves never to steal cigarettes again.

Yes/No

Scenario 2

A young man is out for the night drinking with his mates. He gets into a fight with two other young men, but manages to defend himself against them. His mates are impressed with the way he handles himself and spread the story of his fighting expertise widely. Now, when he goes out on the town, he is singled out by other men looking for a fight and he regularly has to defend himself.

Yes/No

Scenario 3

A 14-year-old girl has done well in her SATs examination, but has little interest in school. However, her teachers have high expectations of her and continually praise her in front of her classmates and friends. She is teased by her peer group about being 'teacher's pet' and begins to miss classes rather than face the teasing. She does reasonably well in her GCSEs, but her teachers are slightly disappointed in her level of performance. She leaves school at 16.

Yes/No

Scenario 4

A young woman has the ambition to be an architect and has achieved good grades in AS art, A level physics, maths, and design. The careers adviser has suggested that she go to university to study art history as she is good at drawing. Her parents are reluctant to support her in going to university as she would be the first female from the family to do so. Her boyfriend is keen to marry and start a family. She takes a year out to think about what she wants to do and gets a good job in a local office. Her ambition to become an architect is put on hold with the birth of her first baby.

Yes/No

Alternative concept: ....

Sick role

Complete the table below by stating two rights and two obligations associated with the sick role.

(a) Rights	(b) Obligations
1	1 ....
2	2 ....

Signification

Suggest a product for which each of the following scenarios might signify a positive mythological effect in an advertisement. Identify the characteristic that the image is signifying.

Advertising scenario	(a) Product	(b) Signification
1 Cows grazing peacefully in very green fields, on a clear blue sunny day.	....	....
2 Clear water bubbling over a small waterfall, with spring flowers blooming brightly at the water's edge.	....	....
3 A steel chain, tautly spanning a large space and under considerable tension.	....	....

Situational constraints

Below is a list of situational constraints. For each one, explain briefly how it may act as a barrier to escaping from poverty.

1 Being a lone mother with dependent children

....

....

....

....

2 Having poor educational qualifications

....

....

....

....

3 Having a physical disability

....

....

....

....

4 Being in long-term unemployment

....

....

....

....

5 Living on a 'deprived' housing estate

....

....

....

....

Social change

Explain the difference between evolutionary and revolutionary ideas of social change.

....

....

....

Social class

Explain the difference between the following pairs.

1 social class – occupational class

....

....

....

2 working class – underclass

....

....

....

3 class-in-itself – class-for-itself

....

....

....

4 proletarianisation – embourgeoisement

....

....

....

5 class culture – class interest

....

....

....

Social closure

Complete the following by identifying the particular form of social closure described.

1 Restricting access by specifying the need for particular qualifications.   ....

2 Trying to ensure that no other group can achieve the same rewards.   ....

3 Using collective action to gain rewards only for members.   ....

Social construction

Place the following social processes in the correct sequence to illustrate the social construction of criminal justice statistics by social agencies. For each process identify two factors that affect this social construction.

....   Conviction   (a) ....
                      (b) ....

....   Reporting   (a) ....
                      (b) ....

....   Discovery   (a) ....
                      (b) ....

....   Sentencing   (a) ....
                       (b) ....

....   Prosecution   (a) ....
                        (b) ....

....   Investigation   (a) ....
                          (b) ....

....   Recording   (a) ....
                      (b) ....

....   Arrest   (a) ....
                   (b) ....

Social control

Distinguish between the following pairs of concepts to do with social control.

1 **(a)** Conformity

....

....

....

(b) Dissent

....

....

....

2 **(a)** Compliance

....

....

....

(b) Resistance

....

....

....

3 **(a)** Sanctions

....

....

....

(b) Rewards

....

....

....

4 **(a)** Morality

....

....

....

(b) Utilitarianism

....

....

....

5 **(a)** Enforced obedience

....

....

....

(b) Commitment

....

....

....

Social facts

Complete the following sentences.

1 Social facts are ways of acting and ....

2 They are .... to the individual.

3 They exercise .... over the individual.

4 Some 'social facts' are social ...., while others are beliefs and ways of ....

5 Durkheim believed that social facts should be studied by sociologists as though they were 'objects' – a view known as ....

Social mobility

Explain the difference between the following terms.

1 social mobility   geographical mobility

....

....

....

....

2 long-range social mobility   short-range social mobility

....

....

....

....

3 intergenerational social mobility   intragenerational social mobility

....

....

....

....

Social order

Complete the following paragraph, using appropriate sociological concepts or terms in place of the numbers.

Social order is seen by sociologists as consisting of **1** .... or patterns of behaviour in society. The **2** .... in particular focus on the issue of social order, seeing it as essential for the achievement of social **3** .... Without social order, society would disintegrate into anarchy, as individuals committed **4** .... to gain what they desired. By establishing social order, societies make social life **5** .... , and it is this that allows individuals to act reasonably towards each other.

Social policy

Identify two links between sociology and social policy.

1 ....

....

2 ....

....

Social selection explanation

Give three criticisms of the 'social selection' explanation of social class differences in health.

1 ....
....

2 ....
....

3 ....
....

Social structure

Fill in the blanks in the passage below.

Structural functionalists view society as a system composed of interlocking

1 .... Each of these has a variety of 2 .... , one of the most

important being its contribution to the 3 .... of the whole social system.

Members of society hold a variety of social 4 .... , e.g. in the family, in the

economic sphere and so on. Each social position has its own 5 .... , or

6 .... ways of behaving. These are learned through the process of

7 ....

Socialisation

Which of the following activities would you identify as being mainly primary socialisation and which as mainly secondary socialisation?

1 Learning to read and write   Primary/Secondary

2 Learning basic values   Primary/Secondary

3 Learning to speak   Primary/Secondary

4 Learning to handle emotions   Primary/Secondary

5 Learning number   Primary/Secondary

6 Learning a trade   Primary/Secondary

Sociology as a science

State whether each of the following statements is true or false.

1 Natural scientists always follow the hypothetico-deductive method of research. ....

2 Natural scientists generally look for 'laws'. ....

3 Natural scientists always use the experimental method. ....

4 Sociologists who try to follow the methods of the natural sciences are known as interpretivists. ....

5 Science is concerned with both the theoretical and the empirical. ....

6 Science is regarded as a rational enterprise, that is, based on logic. ....

7 It is possible to achieve total objectivity in scientific research. ....

8 Human behaviour is meaningful behaviour – humans act as well as react. ....

9 Sociologists try to conduct their research in an objective and systematic manner. ....

10 Sociology is not a 'natural science' but can be regarded as a science. ....

State

Complete the following by briefly describing the view of the state held by each of the different perspectives.

1 Marxist

....

....

2 Weberian

....

....

3 Pluralist

....

....

Status

Decide whether each of these attributes indicates an ascribed or an achieved status. If any are difficult to decide, write down why this is the case.

1 Your gender   ....

2 Your A levels   ....

3 Your driving licence ....

4 Your colour   ....

5 Your clothes   ....

6 Your job   ....

7 Your class of origin ....

8 Your religion   ....

9 Your voting choice   ....

10 Your sexuality   ....

Stratification

Identify two similarities and two differences in the Marxist and Weberian view of stratification in society.

1 **Similarities**

(a) ....

(b) ....

2 **Differences**

(a) ....

(b) ....

Street crime

Street crime is the most visible form of crime (mugging, robbery etc.) and has led to 'realist' theories of crime from both the Marxists and the New Right. For each of these two approaches, complete the boxes, according to the categories in the left-hand column.

	(a) Right realists	(b) Left realists
1 Causes of crime		
2 Nature of the perpetrators of crime		
3 Role of the state in the fight against crime		
4 Solutions to crime		

Strike statistics

Place the following events in the correct order to illustrate the social construction of strike statistics.

(a) Management informed of grievance. ....

(b) Management reports stoppage to government. ....

(c) Management takes no action. ....

(d) Workers down tools while discussion with management goes on. ....

(e) Workers walk out. ....

(f) Grievance amongst workers emerges. ....

(g) Management gives ultimatum to workers to return to work. ....

(h) Workers get union backing for stoppage. ....

(i) Management takes workers off the clock. ....

Subculture

Identify and explain four examples of the way that youth subcultures may distinguish themselves from mainstream society, using the categories below.

Dress ....

....

....

Language ....

....

....

Values ....

....

....

Behaviour ....

....

....

Subjective poverty

Write a brief definition of each of the concepts below, then use them to write a brief paragraph explaining what is meant by subjective poverty.

1 Norms ....

....

2 Poverty line ....

....

3 Reference group ....

....

....

4 Relative deprivation ....

....

5 Status ....

....

....

Subjectivity

Which of the following phrases are connected to subjectivity and which are not?

1 Taking the natural attitude   ....

2 Putting aside one's beliefs   ....

3 Suspending preconceptions   ....

4 Choosing detachment   ....

5 Choosing a side to be on   ....

6 To wear your heart on your sleeve   ....

7 Taking things for granted   ....

Suicide

Identify the appropriate concept from the following for the reasons for suicide in the list.

Egoistic Altruistic Anomic Fatalistic Escapist Aggressive Ludic Oblative

1 Directed towards gaining revenge against others.   ....

2 Too little regulation, not enough social cohesion.   ....

3 Directed towards a moral goal.   ....

4 Too little integration, not enough social cohesion.   ....

5 Directed towards both life and death.   ....

6 Too much regulation, not enough social cohesion.   ....

7 Too much social cohesion, too much integration.   ....

8 Directed towards avoiding further pain or anguish.   ....

Surveillance

Distinguish between the following pairs of concepts, drawn from Foucault's work on surveillance.

1 **(a)** Surveillance

....

....

....

(b) Self-surveillance

....

....

....

2 **(a)** Disciplinary techniques

....

....

....

(b) Anatomo-politics

....

....

....

3 **(a)** Categorisation

....

....

....

(b) Examination

....

....

....

Symmetrical family

Define the following terms from the sociology of the family.

1 Symmetrical family

....
....
....

2 Privatisation

....
....
....

3 Asymmetrical family

....
....
....

4 Egalitarian family

....
....
....

5 Stratified diffusion

....
....
....

Taxation

Fill in the blanks using the words at the end.

1 .... is one of the main ways in which governments raise money. It can be a powerful mechanism in the **2** .... of both **3** .... and **4** .... **5** .... taxation refers to taxes levied directly on a person's wealth or income, such as income tax or **6** .... tax. **7** .... taxation refers to taxes on goods and **8** .... Direct taxation is known as a **9** .... tax, as the more a person has, the more they pay. Indirect taxation, however, such as **10** .... , is known as a **11** .... tax, as by being a flat-rate tax, it takes a greater proportion of the income of the **12** .... than of the **13** ....

**direct   income   indirect   inheritance   poor   progressive   redistribution
regressive   rich   services   taxation   VAT   wealth**

Technological determinism

Define technological determinism using your own words and offer two arguments in favour of the idea and two against.

Definition

(A) Arguments in favour	(B) Arguments against
I	I ....
....	....
....	....
2	2 ....
....	....
....	....

Text

Suggest five media products whose messages can be read as a text, that is, which contain encoded messages to be decoded by the audience.

1 ....

2 ....

3 ....

4 ....

5 ....

Theory

Briefly explain what is meant by a theory.

....

....

....

Third World

The use of the term 'Third World' has been criticised by many sociologists. Offer four such criticisms, using the clues provided as pointers.

Clue 1 – stereotyping   Clue 3 – hierarchy of terms
Clue 2 – overarching concept   Clue 4 – separation

Criticism 1 ....

....

Criticism 2 ....

....

Criticism 3 ....

....

Criticism 4 ....

....

Tiger economies

1 *Identify three government policies pursued by the 'tiger economies' that have contributed to their rapid development, according to the neo-liberals.*

   ....

   ....

   ....

2 *Identify three features of the 'tiger economies' that have contributed to the set-backs they experienced in the 1990s.*

   ....

   ....

   ....

Transnational companies

TNCs are controversial in sociology, with some arguing that they bring great benefits to both the rich and poor countries of the world, and others who argue that their operations are detrimental to both of these. Suggest one benefit and one negative aspect of the activities of the TNCs for both the rich and poor countries of the world.

	(a) Benefit	(b) Cost
I Rich countries	....	....
2 Poor countries	....	....

Underachievement

Give three possible reasons for the educational underachievement of some members of each of the following social groups.

1 Boys

(a) ....

....

....

(b) ....

....

....

(c) ....

....

....

2 Working class

(a) ....

....

....

(b) ....

....

....

(c) ....

....

....

3 Some ethnic minority groups

(a) ....

....

....

(b) ....

....

....

(c) ....

....

....

Underclass

List five characteristics which, according to New Right writers such as Charles Murray, are features of the 'underclass', then give five criticisms which can be made of the concept as used by such writers.

Characteristics of the 'underclass':

1 ....
....

2 ....
....

3 ....
....

4 ....
....

5 ....
....

Criticisms of the concept:

1 ....
....

2 ....
....

3 ....
....

4 ....
....

5 ....
....

Underdevelopment

Answer the following questions about the process of underdevelopment.

1   Before colonialisation, many Third World countries had developed industrial sectors. Give one example of such industries.

    ....

    ....

2   Under colonial rule, much of the wealth of the colonised countries was expropriated by the colonisers. Suggest two ways in which this was done directly.

    ....

    ....

3   Explain the role of the 'terms of trade' in destroying original industries in colonised countries.

    ....

    ....

    ....

4   In the post-colonial era, suggest two ways in which profits made in the Third World are 'patriated' to the First World.

    ....

    ....

    ....

5   Underdevelopment theory suggests that the lack of development is not a natural state. What is the overarching cause of this state, according to dependency theorists?

    ....

    ....

Unemployment

How do the following factors affect unemployment levels? For each factor offer an optimistic and a pessimistic view.

Factor	(a) Optimistic effect	(b) Pessimistic effect
1 Government employment policies		
2 Changes in technology		
3 Globalisation		
4 Workings of the market		

Unitary elite theory

Briefly state three criticisms of unitary elite theory.

1 ....

....

2 ....

....

3 ....

....

Universality of the family

It has been argued that some form of family is an essential requirement for society to exist and persist.

(A) *Identify three 'irreducible' functions that have been proposed as needing a family to perform, regardless of the other structures in society.*

1 ....

2 ....

3 ....

(B) *Offer three criticisms of the idea that the family has to be universal.*

1 ....

2 ....

3 ....

Upper class

Fill in the blanks in the following paragraph by using the words given in the list below.

Traditionally, the term 'upper class' refers to members of the **1** .... Their wealth and titles are **2** .... , being passed down through the generations, and rest on their ownership of **3** .... , hence their being referred to as the '**4** .... gentry'. According to some, the upper class form an **5** .... group in society, with the power to protect and further their own **6** .... at the expense of others. Since the end of the Second World War, the power **7** .... of the upper class has altered, and the group now contains some whose wealth derives from their **8** .... interests. However, wealth alone does not mean that someone will be included in the upper class. Lottery winners, for example, may be **9** .... , but will lack the economic and **10** .... power, as well as the **11** .... , associated with the upper class.

**base   land   business   political   hereditary   elite   landed
interests   wealthy   aristocracy   status**

Urbanisation

Complete the left-hand sentences by matching with the half sentences on the right.

1   Urbanisation plays a central role in modernisation theory because

(A) cities create Gesellschaft rather than Gemeinschaft.

2   Urbanisation represents a change in solidarity in society because

(B) cities can be colonial outposts as well as centres of innovation.

3   Urbanisation undermines traditional values because

(C) cities allow an escape from the restrictions of rural living and give new opportunities to their inhabitants.

4   Cities are important to dependency theory because

(D) cities emphasise universalism over particularism.

5   Urbanisation is not always associated with development because

(E) cities are a vital link between the First World and Third World hinterlands.

Validity

Though a desirable feature of sociological research, validity is difficult to establish in practice. Suggest three reasons why this might be so.

1 ....

....

2 ....

....

3 ....

....

Values

Values are important elements in society, as they act as guides to action. Functionalists argue that they are central to an understanding of social order, through the concept of value-consensus. Write a paragraph of no more than 100 words, which describes what is meant by a value-consensus, why it is seen as important and how it has been criticised.

....

....

....

....

....

....

....

....

....

....

....

Victim-blaming

Below are five suggested causes of poverty. For each one, indicate whether it falls into the category of 'victim-blaming' or not.

1   Being in ill-health   Yes/No

2   Having a large family   Yes/No

3   Living in an area of high unemployment   Yes/No

4   Suffering from racial discrimination in employment   Yes/No

5   Lacking positive attitudes to work   Yes/No

Victim studies

Offer a definition of the following concepts, which are all to do with the study of the victim. For each concept, write a sentence that states an important aspect of it.

Concept	Definition	Importance
1 Victim studies	(a)..	(b)..
2 Multiple victimisation	(a)..	(b)..
3 Victim proneness	(a)..	(b)..
4 Victim precipitation	(a)..	(b)..
5 Fear of crime	(a)..	(b)..

Wealth

1   *Explain the difference between 'wealth' and 'marketable wealth'.*

....

....

....

....

2   *Study the table below and answer the questions.*

Distribution of marketable wealth *excluding* the value of dwellings: United Kingdom 1976–1996 (percentages)

% of wealth owned by:	1976	1981	1986	1991	1995	1996
Wealthiest 1%	29	26	25	29	28	27
Wealthiest 5%	47	45	46	51	51	50
Wealthiest 10%	57	56	58	64	64	63
Wealthiest 25%	73	74	75	80	81	82
Wealthiest 50%	88	87	89	93	93	94

(Source: Social Trends 30, ONS 2000)

(a) By how many percentage points did the marketable wealth of the wealthiest 5% of the population change between 1976 and 1996?

....

(b) Which group showed the greatest increase in its share of marketable wealth between 1986 and 1996?

....

(c) What percentage of marketable wealth was owned by the least wealthy 90% of the population in 1996?

....

(d) What was the percentage share of marketable wealth of the poorest 50% of the population in 1976?

....

(e) What was the percentage share of marketable wealth of the poorest 50% of the population in 1996?

....

Welfare

For each of the areas of life listed below, give an example of a social policy designed to improve or ensure the welfare of citizens.

1 Family ....

2 Education ....

3 Work ....

4 Health ....

5 Old age ....

Welfare dependency

Give five examples of groups of people who may be entirely dependent on welfare benefits for their income.

1 ....

2 ....

3 ....

4 ....

5 ....

Welfare State

The sentences below represent different opinions regarding the Welfare State. Indicate which statement belongs with which perspective.

Statement	Perspective
1 The Welfare State serves as an instrument of control over women, with its historical emphasis on women's dependency on men, and by emphasising women's role as primary carers.	**(A)** Marxist
2 Some degree of state welfare provision is necessary and desirable to deal with some of the social problems likely to arise from a capitalist free market economy, e.g. low wages and unemployment, and also to involve people as citizens.	**(B)** New Right
3 The Welfare State meets the needs of capitalism for a healthy workforce and also, by presenting the welfare system as fair and just, perpetuates ruling-class ideology.	**(C)** New Labour
4 State welfare provision should be kept to the absolute minimum, as too much state intervention interferes with the free play of market forces and encourages welfare dependency.	**(D)** Social democratic
5 Welfare is not about a safety net or a handout, but about helping people to help themselves and widening participation in employment.	**(E)** Feminist

Work

In the following categorisation, place the examples in an appropriate location. Note that some activities might be better placed across categories.

**cleaning your own house   cooking a meal in a bed-and-breakfast
barbecuing in your garden   getting the bus to the office
driving a bus   ironing a shirt to wear at a meeting   playing basketball
teaching your child to talk   teaching in a classroom   having a pint
reading an official report at home   busking**

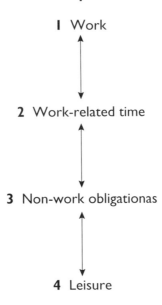

1 Work

2 Work-related time

3 Non-work obligationas

4 Leisure

Work satisfaction

Match up the ideas on the left with the theorists on the right who are mainly associated with them, by drawing arrows.

1 Self-actualisation	**(A)** Maslow
2 Hierarchy of need	**(B)** Mayo
3 Motivations to work	**(C)** Argyris
4 Piece work	**(D)** Baldamus
5 Human capital	**(E)** Goldthorpe and Lockwood
6 Instrumentalism	**(F)** Taylor
7 Traction	**(G)** Herzberg

Working class

1   *The paragraph below contains a number of stereotypes of the working class. Briefly indicate why these stereotypes are inaccurate, and cannot be applied generally to members of the working class.*

> Working-class people work in unskilled manual occupations where they earn high wages. They have large families and live in council houses in inner-city areas. They read the Sun newspaper and vote Labour, and those in work belong to a trade union. Working-class children fail at school and go on to become unemployed or unskilled manual workers like their fathers.

....

....

....

....

....

....

....

....

....

....

....

....

....

....

....

....

....

....

continued

2   *State briefly what is meant by the following:*

(a) privatised working class

....

....

....

....

(b) affluent working class

....

....

....

....

(c) deferential working class

....

....

....

....

(d) new working class

....

....

....

....

(e) old working class

....

....

....

....

World Systems Theory

Complete the following quiz on World Systems Theory. Each answer is possible using only one word.

1 Who is the main sociologist who proposed the idea of World Systems Theory?   ....

2 In which year was his main work first published?   ....

3 What was the concept he applied to the main exploiting countries in the world system?   ....

4 Countries that were exploited and exploited others in turn were called what?   ....

5 From where did he argue that capital was patriated back to the exploiting countries of the world?   ....

6 What type of economy did he argue influenced the affairs of all nation-states?   ....

7 What type of division of labour did he see as most important?   ....

8 What dimension of property relationships did he see as determinant?   ....

9 Which mainstream sociological perspective is he usually associated with?   ....

10 What type of value was crucial for the exploitation of the world's resources?   ....

A-Z Answers

Absolute poverty

Absolute poverty is defined as lacking the basic necessities such as food, warmth, shelter and access to health care. While this kind of poverty is indeed associated with some developing countries, the existence of a considerable number of homeless people in Britain indicates that absolute poverty can still be found here.

Action

1 actions; 2 structures; 3 situations; 4 external; 5 create; 6 socialisation; 7 expectations; 8 actions; 9 subjective; 10 systems

Affluent workers

1(a) **Affluent working class** Manual workers working in the high wage sectors such as car assembly and who were seen in the 1960s as constituting a new type of worker.

1(b) **Instrumental working class** Often associated with affluence, these were workers at all levels of income who were interested in money rather than class issues, in terms of their identity and actions.

2(a) **Embourgeoisement** The process whereby it was claimed that affluent sections of the working class were becoming middle class in terms of their consumption patterns, behaviour and identities.

2(b) **Proletarianisation** The process whereby it was claimed that routinised middle-class workers were becoming like the working class in terms of trade union identification, actions and attitudes.

3(a) **Privatised working class** The section of the working class, usually affluent, who were seen as spending more of their leisure time in the home rather than in solidaristic leisure such as going out with their workmates.

3(b) **Traditional working class** Usually identified with heavy manual work, this group had solidaristic ideologies, reflected in leisure activities based around workmates and with a strong socialist ideology.

4(a) **Incorporation thesis** The process whereby it was claimed that affluent workers were being absorbed into capitalist structures so that they no longer posed a challenge to them.

4(b) **Immiseration thesis** The process whereby it was claimed that the working class would increasingly be impoverished by capitalism so that they would eventually revolt against it.

5(a) **Aristocracy of labour** The group of highly skilled workers, who were usually more highly paid than others and who were therefore concerned to protect their differential pay from erosion by those workers they felt were inferior in skill.

5(b) **Lumpenproletariat** The group of unorganised workers, who were poorly paid and who were constantly striving to survive. They were often associated with petty law-breaking and a lack of identity with other sections of the working class.

Age

1 **Age dependency** Where some age groups rely on others to give them support and maintain them. The two main dependent age groups are young people who are either pre-school, still at school or in higher education, and the old who have retired from gainful employment. These are dependent on the working population, situated between the two groups.

2 **Gerontocracy** Where the old are revered as having wisdom on account of their experience and who therefore hold power in society. Traditional Chinese society was a gerontocracy.

3 **Generation** A social group, usually identified as spanning roughly 30 years, who therefore inhabit the same historical interlude, and who can be said to have roughly similar experiences. They are often defined around important historical events or watersheds, such as the post-war generation.

4 **Third age** Used to describe the age range between 50 and the mid-70s, which covers the period when most people will have completed bringing up their families and move onto retirement. The affluence of the late 20th century meant that many third agers had surplus income and surplus time. They thus became an important consumer category.

5 **Youth subculture** Used to denote the distinctiveness of certain groups of young people from mainstream society, in terms of their life-styles, attitudes and values. Prominent youth subcultures in the second half of the 20th century ranged from teddy boys, through hippies to punk rockers. They are often linked to particular social classes or ethnic groups.

Age-set

1 A concept particularly associated with traditional societies
2 A group of people of the same age (often used to refer specifically to males)
3 The group usually undergoes a 'rite de passage' to pass from one status group to another

Agenda-setting

1 **Copy typist:** No. Copy typists only word process into the machines copy which has been decided by others
2 **Journalist:** Yes. Journalists can influence public debate through the way that they write up stories.
3 **Editor:** Yes. Editors can influence which stories are made prominent through headlining or sidelining particular issues.
4 **Printer:** No. Printers have no input into the way that the news is presented.
5 **Owner:** Yes or No. Some sociologists argue that owners can directly intervene to make stories more prominent, or to have them 'spiked'. Others would argue that owners have no direct influence on the day-to-day production of the news.

Aid

1 **Marxist: A** Imperialism by the back door. **B** This suggests that aid is used as a way of maintaining the dominance of the First World over poor countries. **C** Implies that all aid is a con trick and not genuinely aimed at helping Third World countries develop their economies.
2 **Social Democratic: A** Intermediate technology. **B** This suggests that aid is best spent not on large-scale projects which benefit providers as well as recipients, but on smaller developments. **C** Ignores the benefits of large-scale projects which, for example, bring electricity or water to millions.
3 **New Right: A** Dependency culture. **B** This suggests that aid creates a sense of obligation by recipients, so that they come to expect support from the First World automatically, rather than solving problems themselves. **C** Leads ultimately to non provision of aid and negative consequences for those who would have been in receipt of it.

Alienation

1 used the machinery to separate out individual workers; 2 characterised by different machines; 3 focus on their own tasks and ignore other aspects; 4 has to learn the tasks associated with that machine; 5 have no choice; 6 most workers have little commitment to work

Allocation process

(a) and 3; (b) and 1; (c) and 5; (d) and 4; (e) and 2

Allocative control

1 The owners of organisations.
2 Strategic planning.
3 The power to decide which parts of the organisation receive more or less funding; the ability to write the mission statement/business plan of the organisation; to determine the overall direction of the organisation; to set targets for performance of the organisation as a whole; to identify the goals of an organisation.
4 Board of Directors.
5 Members may lose their jobs if fewer resources are allocated to their section; members may have fewer support structures if resources are cut; members' career prospects may be enhanced if greater funds are allocated to their areas etc.

Anomie

Durkheim – Anomie, Interdependence of inter-related parts, Organic solidarity
Marx – Alienation, Forces of production, Exploitation
Weber – Verstehen, Ideal type, Rational action

Artefact explanation

1 – D; 2 – C; 3 – A; 4 – B

Authority

1 Authority; 2 Both; 3 Power; 4 Power; 5 Both;
6 Authority

Automation

1 That automation will reduce the number of workers needed.
2 That automation will change the skills that workers will need in the workplace.
3 That fewer hours of work will be needed as routine operations are done by machines.
4 That hierarchies will be flattened as routine control functions are carried out by computers.
5 That more co-operative working will be needed to deal with the complex technologies.
6 Computer experts will become very powerful, as they provide the underlying support to expert systems.
7 Physical prowess will become less valued, as machines take over the burden of production.
8 That the new machines will serve to separate workers from each other, as extreme specialisation results.
9 That computers will determine how fast is the production of goods.
10 Growth of 'just-in-time' production as computers manage stocks more efficiently.

Body

1 physical; 2 social; 3 construct; 4 societies;
5 pure; 6 demons; 7 post-modernists; 8 discourses;
9 body; 10 shape; 11 feminists; 12 pressures;
13 eating; 14 disorders; 15 bulimia; 16 anorexia;
17 nervosa.

Bureaucracy

1   Ideal type
2   Informal organisation
3   Situational rules or rules-in-use
4   People
5   The body
6   McDonaldisation
7   Dysfunctional
8   Oligarchy
9   Organismic organisations
10   Total organisations

Caste

1 Caste, Estate; 2 Caste, Estate; 3 Caste; 4 Class;
5 Estate; 6 Caste; 7 Class; 8 Estate; 9 Caste;
10 Caste, Class; 11 Caste, Estate; 12 Caste, Estate,
Class; 13 Class

Cheque book voting

Cheque book voting refers to a particular kind of
instrumental voting, in which voters are particularly
influenced by the likely effects of a party's policies on
their disposable income, particularly as a result of policies
on **taxation**. The existence and possible increase of such
voters has made it increasingly difficult for **opinion polls**
to predict accurately the outcome of general elections.
This is because when voters are asked what things are
important to them, they tend to focus on **public issues**
such as health, crime and education. However, when they
come to cast their vote, they are more swayed by
concerns of **private prosperity**, and are most likely to
vote for the party they believe will give them more
money in their pocket.

Childhood

1   While the state of being a child is related to the age
    a person is, it is also related to how society defines
    when a young person becomes an adult. Childhood is
    therefore socially constructed.
2   Through legislation, the state determines when young
    people are allowed to do certain things, such as
    smoke, drink alcohol, fight in the army etc.
3   Some sociologists argue that until the Victorian era,
    society saw the young as little adults, with no
    separate category of childhood existing.
4   Individual responsibility for criminal acts is defined in
    an age-related way. In the past, youngsters were seen
    as entirely responsible for their criminal activity and

were processed as adults. Increasingly society
differentiates between those who are too young to
know what they are doing is wrong, those who have
a diminished responsibility because of their age and
those who have full responsibility. The age at which
these categories operate is defined in law.
5   Just because a young person is physically mature
    (which is happening earlier because of better diet
    etc.) does not necessarily mean they have the
    experience to take full responsibility for their actions.

Church

1   Bureaucratically and hierarchically structured
2   Holds/supports conservative values
3   Supports the established order of society
4   Wide membership – usually by ascription
5   A well-established religious body

Church attendance statistics

1   The statistics sometimes relate to the number of
    attendances on one particular occasion, such as
    Easter Day services.
2   People may hold religious beliefs even if they do not
    attend church services.
3   In some surveys, double-counting occurs, i.e. the same
    people may attend both morning and evening
    services, and thus be counted twice.

Clash of cultures

1   **Clash of cultures** It suggests that all schools and all
    children of ethnic minority groups are the same,
    ignoring important differences between them. By
    focusing on the home background, it underestimates
    the importance of social processes within schools.
2   **Black box view** This takes for granted what goes on
    in schools, and focuses on the home background or
    the wider society, thus ignoring a significant factor in
    explaining underachievement among some groups.
3   **Language** It assumes that all underachieving children
    from ethnic minority groups do not have English as a
    first language, and ignores the fact that many have
    been born and reared in Britain and are completely
    fluent in the language.

Class boundaries debate

Possible criticisms are:
1   The groups are too large; significant differences are
    found within the group labelled the proletariat; people
    may have significant amounts of power without
    necessarily owning the means of production.
2   If the distinction between the middle and working
    class is based on non-manual/manual occupations,
    what is the basis of the difference between the
    middle and upper class? Again, there are significant
    differences within the groups.

3 Allocation usually based on the occupation of the male partner; ranking fails to take into account factors such as degree of autonomy, working conditions and prospects; does not include those without employment.

Class structure

Possible changes include:
1. The decrease in the proportion of the workforce in manual and manufacturing jobs, therefore a decline in 'the working class'.
2. The increase in the number of people working in the service sector, therefore more people in 'middle-class occupations'.
3. An increase in two-income families
4. An increase in the number of families with no wage-earners.
5. Some increase in social mobility.

Classroom interaction

One way would be as follows: Sociologists taking an **interactionist** perspective do not believe that a focus on children's home background offers a satisfactory explanation of differential educational achievement. They believe that it is what goes on in classrooms that is important. They believe that classroom interaction is a **negotiated process** between teacher and pupils, and that we need to uncover the **meanings** held by each group to understand what is going on. For example, the **peer group** is a powerful force in classrooms, and many aspects of pupils' behaviour is a result of a desire to conform to the norms of their peer group. Similarly, teachers may hold **negative stereotypes** of some children or groups, and this will affect their behaviour towards them.

Cohabitation

1. **Cohabitation** is an unmarried couple living in the same household, usually engaged in a sexual relationship. **Marriage** is a legal state of union between a woman and a man. **Same sex couples** are where two people of the same sex live together, usually in a sexual relationship.
2. **Divorce** is the legal end to a marriage, determined by a court. **Marital breakdown** is where relationships between a married couple have disintegrated, though they may still live in the same household. **Separation** is a legal state, where the couple are recognised as being apart, while still legally married.
3. **Adoption** is a legal process whereby a couple or an individual is recognised as responsible for a child. **Fostering** is a temporary arrangement whereby a

child in the care of the state is looked after by responsible adults. **Voluntary childlessness** is the choice that some couples make not to have any children of their own or through adoption or fostering.

Collectivism

Collectivism with regard to welfare is a view which states that welfare should be delivered by the state to all citizens as a right of citizenship, while **individualism** is a view which regards the individual as primarily responsible for providing for his/her welfare, with state involvement, if any, acting as a 'safety-net'.

Colonialism

The legacy of colonialism can be seen most clearly in the **national boundaries** left in Africa and parts of Asia. These boundaries did not follow natural linguistic or ethnic borders, but were established, either as a result of the rivalries between different **colonial powers**, or as an administrative convenience for the colonising power.

As a result the post-colonial nations are often divided by ethnic, religious, tribal or **language** differences. Under colonialism, the tactic of **divide-and-rule** was employed to exploit these divisions, but they have often left a legacy of bitterness between different groups within the same state. The colonising power also tried to strip away the identity of the groups under their control by undermining their traditional **customs** or by denying them access to their history. Thus, the **history** of a society became its history since the arrival of the coloniser. Anything worthwhile beforehand was not acknowledged. The legacy is continued in the **trading relationships** often established between the ex-coloniser and ex-colony, in which the latter continues to be exploited by the former. This situation is known as **neo-colonialism**. However, there are more positive aspects to the legacy as many former colonies identify with the **community of nations** formed during the **decolonisation** period, united as they are by a common history and language, albeit imposed by the colonising nation.

Compensatory education

1 United States; 2 failure; 3 lower; 4 ethnic;
5 minority; 6 home; 7 background; 8 disadvantaged;
9 education; 10 compensatory; 11 education;
12 Head; 13 Start; 14 difficult; 15 IQ; 16 catch-up;
17 improvement; 18 cultural; 19 deprivation;
20 culture; 21 middle 22 class; 23 upbringing;
24 structural; 25 standards; 26 self-fulfilling;
27 prophecy

Comprehensivisation

Note that some of the reasons for and against seem to contradict each other. This reflects the differing beliefs of those who hold the views.

Reasons in favour

1 Under the tri-partite system, selection was not based on merit.
2 Eleven is too young an age at which to decide a child's educational future.
3 Children will mix with others from a variety of social backgrounds.
4 Under the tri-partite system, there were wide differences in status between the different types of school, with children in secondary modern schools being regarded as 'failures'.
5 Children have access to the full curriculum.
6 Evidence shows that brighter children do not suffer, and that less-gifted children do better when taught in comprehensive schools.

Reasons against

1 Brighter children benefit from being taught in groups of children of similar ability to themselves.
2 Selective schools allow children to be taught in specialist schools catering for their particular types of ability, e.g. musical, scientific, artistic.
3 Comprehensive schools are 'neighbourhood' schools, therefore some of them will be 'sink' schools.

Conflict

1 consensus; 2 material; economic; 3 bourgeoisie; proletariat; 4 class; 5 stability (or order)

Conglomeration

1 – C; 2 – B; 3 – A

Conjugal roles

1 **Power/decision-making: A** While the wife may have power over certain areas, important decisions such as location would be determined by the husband's career. **B** Important decisions would be negotiated from a situation of equality, with the wife's job being as important as the husband's in location.
2 **Domestic division of labour: A** The prime responsibility for housework would be the wife's and the husband would have the area of house maintenance, garden, etc. **B** The husband would have an equal commitment to the routine chores of domestic labour and the wife would be involved in bigger projects.
3 **Responsibility for childcare: A** The wife would take primary responsibility for the children, though decisions such as schooling would be taken by the husband. **B** Both parents would be concerned with the day-to-day care of children and in larger decisions about their lives, such as schooling.

4 **Relationships with rest of the family: A** The wife would usually maintain routine relationships with both sides of the family. **B** Husbands would take responsibility for contact with their side of the family.
5 **Social life: A** The wife's social life would be family-centred, the husband's focused on work and friends in the public sphere. **B** Social life would be home-centred with activities carried out together.

These descriptions cannot capture the full complexity of family life. While there are commonalities in family life, each family has differences from these ideal types. In particular, the descriptions of joint conjugal roles offer an ideological view of family life. In reality, any move towards equality is complex, multi-faceted and by no means complete. Feminists have argued that, while there have undoubtedly been changes in conjugal roles, men still retain control over the important decisions to be made.

Consensus

Consensus refers to agreement based on shared values, whereas hegemony refers to a manufactured or manipulated agreement from the working class, who subscribe to values not in their interest because they are persuaded to do so by ruling-class ideology.

Consumption

Sociological interest in **consumption** has coincided with an increasing interest in the issue of **leisure**. Some sociologists have argued that we now live in a **leisure society**, where leisure becomes much more important than **social class**, as a mean of constructing our **identities**. Consumption has therefore become an important **social indicator**, defining individual **life-styles** and engaging people in that most **postmodern** of life's experiences – **shopping**.

Content analysis

1 texts; 2 taken-for-granted assumptions;
3 quantitative; 4 genres; 5 objective; 6 natural attitude; 7 deconstructing; 8 relativism

Core functions of the family

Core functions: 3, 5, 6, 8; **Minor functions:** 1, 2, 4, 7

The minor functions have been taken over by bureaucratic organisations, such as schools, hospitals, churches and companies that have developed with industrialisation.

Correspondence principle

1 Education teaches the basic skills of numeracy and literacy, without which it is difficult to get a job.
2 Schools give praise, high marks, certificates etc. for 'good' work and behaviour, and have a variety of

punishments such as 'lines', detentions, letters home to parents, withdrawal of privileges etc. for 'bad' work and behaviour.

3   Middle-class children are more likely to be educated in schools in middle-class neighbourhoods and to be in higher streams/sets than working-class children. They are more likely to be entered for external examinations and to stay on in education post-16.

4   Middle-class children are less likely to take 'vocational' subjects or courses, and are more likely to be given positions of responsibility at school.

5   Teachers are more likely to hold negative stereotypes of working-class children and regard them as potential 'trouble-makers' who need firm discipline to keep them under control.

Possible criticisms include:

1   Much, if not most, of what is taught in schools is not a direct preparation for work.

2   Given that most people will have more than one kind of job in their working life, a direct relationship between education and work would not be possible – the need is for flexible workers willing and able to undergo training and re-training.

3   There is no consensus among employers regarding what future employees should be taught in school.

4   The nature of work is changing so rapidly that skills taught in school would be out-of-date in a few years.

Crime

1   **(a)** On the stage of a theatre; **(b)** In the street
2   **(a)** United Kingdom; **(b)** Ireland
3   **(a)** Over 18; **(b)** Under 18
4   **(a)** Most places in Great Britain; **(b)** Public buildings in Russia
5   **(a)** In war; **(b)** In peacetime
6   **(a)** United States in the 1970s; **(b)** Singapore in the 1970s
7   **(a)** In the sauna; **(b)** In a public swimming pool
8   **(a)** Boxing ring; **(b)** Disco
9   **(a)** Fox-hunting; **(b)** Cockfighting

Crimes of the powerful

1   **(c)**; Occupational crime is individual, often low level and aimed at benefiting the individual financially at the expense of the organisation for which the individual works. Crimes of the powerful are where the individual uses the power of the organisation which they control for their own private benefit. Corporate crime is carried out by members of the organisation to benefit the organisation, not the individual.

2   **(b)**; Professional crime is where the organisation carries out illegal activities as its main business, even where there may be some legitimate front. Both corporate and occupational crimes occur within organisations whose main activities are legal.

3   **(c)**; Though white-collar crime covers many activities from large-scale fraud to petty pilfering, it is usually used to denote middle-class crime. Both crimes of the powerful and state crime are carried out by powerful individuals associated with the ruling class.

Crimes without victims

1   **(a)** Prostitution; **(b)** Homosexual activity between 17 year olds; **(c)** Smoking marijuana

2   **(a)** Prostitution undermines the family, which is the basis of society; **(b)** Seventeen year olds are too young to engage in sexual activity which is seen by many as deviant; **(c)** It encourages a hedonistic attitude that undermines the work ethic

3   **(a)** Prostitutes may define themselves as service workers providing a necessary outlet for sexual energy; **(b)** If heterosexuals can make the choice at sixteen, then so should homosexuals; **(c)** Marijuana is no more hedonistic than drinking alcohol, which is legal

4   Crimes without victims represent the limits of tolerance by the state and constitute the boundaries between individualism and collective morality

Critical criminology

1 capitalism;   **2** individualism;   **3** acquisitive;
4 property;   **5** socialism

Cultural capital

1   Yes. Can help the child get ahead in IT skills; can give the child access to huge amount of information.

2   No. These might be a sign of wealth and status, but do not give any direct educational advantage.

3   Yes. Many of the concepts and ideas used in education will be familiar, and the child will be able more easily to impress the teachers.

4   Yes. The child is more likely to ask questions when something is not understood, to volunteer answers in class, thus impressing the teachers, and is more likely to be given responsibility.

5   No. Unless the child used the money to buy 'educational' products or to go on school trips, this of itself does not convey educational advantage.

Cultural reproduction

(b) is the correct definition; **(a)** cultural imperialism;
(c) cultural difference theory

Culture

1   (a) An attribute that is given to an individual at birth, such as name and gender. (b) A distinguishing attribute that is gained during secondary socialisation processes, such as educational level.

2   (a) Associated with elite forms of art and entertainment, such as opera, ballet, etc. (b) Associated with mass forms of art and entertainment, such as football or bingo.

3   (a) Where one type of culture is predominant in society and all members are expected to act in accordance with it. (b) Where many cultures exist in society, so that 'bricolage' or borrowing from different cultures is usual.

4   (a) Where tradition is dominant, so little cultural change occurs. (b) Where contemporary culture is open to change, usually amongst peer groups. (c) Where change is rapid and the emphasis is on novelty in cultural forms.

5   (a) Where a culture establishes itself through pervasive effort as the dominant cultural form. (b) Where an alternative culture establishes itself, either separate from or in opposition to hegemonic culture.

Culture of poverty

A1 If a person believes that misfortune is due to 'fate', then they will not try to do anything to escape from it, as they will feel that they are powerless to change things.

A2 Living on state benefits for a long period of time could rob a person of self-confidence, so that they might believe that they were incapable of supporting themselves, and would continue to rely on the state.

A3 If a person is unemployed and does not have the routine of having to get up and go to work each day, they can become listless and lose the will or energy to go out and look for work.

A4 Living in poverty can easily result in depression and feelings of despair, as the person's situation seems hopeless.

A5 Wanting immediate rewards might prevent someone from investing time and possibly money in a training or education course which might improve long-term prospects.

B1 It places the 'blame' for poverty on the individual or family, and thus ignores external factors which may prevent people from escaping from poverty, such as lack of suitable employment opportunities.

B2 There is no empirical evidence to suggest that people would rather remain unemployed and on welfare than in work.

B3 The view ignores the structured inequality built into capitalist society.

Culture structure

1   (a) The methods by which it is legitimate in any society to try to achieve goals. (b) The desired objects of effort in any society, as defined in the culture of any society.

2   (a) The ways in which individuals in a society accommodate to the means and goals of the society. (b) The acceptance of the legitimate means and ends of a society by an individual, which creates the law-abiding citizen.

3   (a) Deviants/criminals who desire the goals of a society but reject the usual means to engage in unlawful activity. (b) Deviants who slavishly follow the means, but who cannot achieve all the goals of a society, limiting their ambition.

4   (a) Deviants who withdraw from mainstream society into subterranean subcultures, such as alcohol abusers. (b) Deviants/criminals who seek to change either means or ends of society, in rejecting the 'game as it stands'.

Curriculum

(a)   The subjects and courses offered in schools and colleges which form pupils' programmes of study.

(b)   The values, beliefs and attitudes which pupils learn informally, and often unknowingly, alongside the formal curriculum.

(c)   The formal programme of study laid down by the Government for all children aged between 5 and 16 being educated in the state system.

(d)   A programme of study in which the knowledge, ideas, attitudes and viewpoints in the various subjects taught are all taken from the perspective of one particular ethnic group, usually the majority group in that society.

(e)   Things such as sport, drama, music and various clubs which take place as optional activities after school hours.

Cycle of poverty

1 – (e);   2 – (d);   3 – (b);   4 – (g);   5 – (a);
6 – (f);   7 – (c)

Dark figure of crime

1 Cartels fixing the price of goods;   2 Prostitution;
3 Burglary;   4 Assault by a spouse;   5 Rape;
6 Petty thefts

Death of the family

1 **(a)** There has been a large increase in divorce indicating that people are no longer happy with life-long marriage.
(b) There has been an increase in cohabitation, which indicates that people are less committed to life-long relationships.
(c) There has been a loss of functions of the family in modern societies, which indicates the decreasing importance of the family.

2 **(a)** Marriage remains as popular as ever, with most divorcees remarrying at some stage.
(b) The lack of a marriage certificate does not necessarily indicate a lack of commitment to a life-long partner, but rather the loss of stigma associated with cohabitation.
(c) The functions of the family have changed rather than declined, and all political parties are keen to be seen as family-friendly. This indicates its continued importance.

Decoding

1 audience; **2** encoded; **3** texts; **4** intentions; **5** selective interpretation

Democracy

Characteristics of representative democracies include:
1 Regular, free and fair elections
2 Universal franchise (one vote for each of those old enough to vote)
3 A free press
4 Freedom of speech
5 Freedom of assembly (the right of people to hold meetings)
6 The existence of opposition parties

Demystification

disengagement
Both demystification and disenchantment refer to the replacement of beliefs in magic and the supernatural by more rational, scientific explanations and modes of thought, while disengagement refers to the separation of church and state.

Denomination

1 Christian; **2** midway; **3** church; **4** sect;
5 well established; **6** social order; **7** formal;
8 wide; **9** stable

Dependency theory

1 – Strength, **2** – Strength, **3** – Strength, **4** – Weakness,
5 – Weakness, **6** – Strength, **7** – Weakness,
8 – Weakness, **9** – Weakness, **10** – Strength

Deskilling

1 – C; **2** – E; **3** – A; **4** – D; **5** – B

Determinism

For Marx, the basis of social behaviour was economic, i.e. the relationship to the means of production. For functionalists, the basis of social behaviour is the shared values learned during the process of socialisation.

Development

1 **(a)** Where industrial production predominates, as a result of processes of urbanisation and industrialisation. **(b)** Where industrial production does not yet predominate in society, and the rural economy is still strong. **(c)** Where previously well-developed societies have been made less developed through their relationships with imperialist countries.

2 **(a)** The view that societies naturally evolve towards a developed state, as a result of slow changes specific to any one society. **(b)** The view that all societies go through the same stages of development towards a fixed end-state. **(c)** The view that all societies are developing the same solutions to the problems of an industrial society and will resemble the United States.

3 **(a)** Changes in the relationships between people consequent upon development. It usually refers to more open and loose relationships. **(b)** Changes in the way that production and consumption are organised consequent upon development. It usually refers to the dominance of factory forms of production. **(c)** Changes in the way that power is organised in society consequent upon development. It usually refers to a more democratic and pluralist form of government.

4 **(a)** The concentration of the population in cities and towns, as a result of the development of industry.
(b) The dispersal of city population to the outskirts, as people search for less crowded, more 'rural-like' living space. **(c)** The flight of urban population to rural areas, creating a commuter population, moving to towns to work by day.

Deviance

Deviance – actions which go against the norm, and which may be criminal or non-criminal.
Social diversion – mild forms of deviance, which are affected by changes in public opinion, as to whether they are deviant or not.
Social deviations – activities that are disapproved of but which some people would like to make illegal.
Conflict crimes – illegal activities about which there is public debate as to whether they should be decriminalised.

Consensus crimes – illegal activities about which there is a general agreement that they should remain so.
Acceptable crimes – illegal activities that are carried out by many in society and which are not generally disapproved of.

Differential association

1 **(a)** Individuals come into contact with pro-law or anti-law attitudes to different degrees. The more anti-law contacts, the greater likelihood of a person becoming a criminal. **(b)** This reduces individuals to being the product of their environment and ignores the choices that individuals can make in committing or not committing crime.

2 **(a)** Each area of a city has a different culture and areas of social disorganisation are likely to have higher crime rates, for example the zone of transition. **(b)** Not all cities have such distinct zones as is implied by the theory, nor does social disorganisation always lead to high crime.

3 **(a)** Cities are characterised by tension between the individual's need for freedom of action and society's need for social control, which leads to greater amounts of crime in urban areas. **(b)** The focus on the city leads to an underestimation of the amount of crime in rural areas, and a switch of police resources to urban locations, leaving the rural population feeling vulnerable.

4 **(a)** The growth of cities into large units means that they subdivide into distinct neighbourhoods, but that meaningful contact amongst neighbours is lessened. **(b)** This tends to stereotype urban dwellers as impersonal and individualistic, offering a pessimistic view of urban life, far from its real excitement.

Disability

Three possible criticisms are:

1 It is a blanket term used to describe a wide range of conditions which differ widely in their consequences.

2 It is a negative and pejorative term which attempts to categorise those affected in terms of what they cannot do in comparison with 'able-bodied' people, thus highlighting their assumed helplessness and dependency.

3 It is at least partly a social construct and as such is as much a political as a medical term.

Discourse

1 – True, 2 – True, 3 – False, 4 – True, 5 – False

Divorce

1 The number of divorces in any one year per thousand married couples in the population.

2 The major reason for these peaks is changes in legislation, which are permissive of divorce; that is, they make divorce easier. Couples trapped in unhappy marriages, because they do not have grounds under existing legislation, will rush to seek a divorce if more lenient laws are introduced.

3 The impact of feminism has helped women to take greater control of their own lives and be more proactive in seeking a divorce.

4 **(a)** Because people are living longer, they would have to spend more time in a marriage than previously. This has increased the strain on married couples. **(b)** Public morality has shifted, so that it is no longer a stigma to be divorced in society's eyes.

5 This is the idea that divorce has consequences for the children of the divorced couple, in terms of a greater likelihood of problems for them later in life.

Domestic economy

1 **(a)** Working in the fields in agriculture near household. Carrying out basic household maintenance. **(b)** Main bread-winner, working outside of household. Carrying out relatively few maintenance activities. **(c)** Working outside household to provide some of family income. More equal contribution to maintenance activities.

2 **(a)** Producing goods to sell in household. Carrying out basic domestic maintenance activities. **(b)** Isolated from productive activity outside of household. Main responsibility for maintenance activity in domestic economy. **(c)** Working outside household to provide income for family. Main responsibility still for domestic maintenance.

3 **(a)** Contributes to domestic economy through labour in household. Carries out maintenance through domestic activities. **(b)** Increasingly isolated from production outside of home. Becoming a cost rather than a contributor to domestic economy. Limited contribution to maintenance tasks. **(c)** Long-term drain on family finance until formal education is completed. Contribution to maintenance activities varied, depending on status of parents.

Domestic labour

1 childcare;   2 capitalism;   3 functions;   4 economy;
5 labour power;   6 biological;   7 peripheral;   8 survival

Drift

1 interactionist;   2 life-cycle;   3 career;   4 status;
5 adulthood;   6 master status;   7 stigmatised

Dual economy thesis

1 underdevelopment; 2 Third World; 3 transnational companies; 4 urban-based; 5 Stock Exchanges; 6 satellites; 7 subsistence; 8 peasant farming; 9 Marxist; 10 exploitation

Ecumenicalism

1 refers to the process in which different Christian religious groups work together co-operatively, such as joint Church of England and Roman Catholic services.

2 refers to the use of television programmes to spread evangelical Christian messages. It is particularly associated with the United States, where some Christian evangelical groups own their own broadcasting networks.

3 refers to a situation in which members of a group believe that there is a mystical relationship between the group and certain objects, such as trees, and worship these objects with particular rituals.

Educational standards

1 educational standards are usually measured by reference to pass rates, that is, the proportion of pupils gaining 'pass grades' in external examinations.

2 in grammar schools, virtually all pupils were entered for external examinations, and the pass rates for those children were quite high.

3 with the comprehensivisation of secondary schooling, pupils from a much wider range of abilities were entered for external examinations, making it difficult to make comparisons between the two systems.

4 as the proportion of pupils gaining exam passes has continued to rise, some have argued that the introduction of coursework has made examinations easier.

5 the introduction of the National Curriculum means that pupils are now tested throughout their school career, at the ages of 7, 11, 13 and 16.

6 schools now have to publish their examination results, with the result that parents can compare the exam results of different schools.

Embourgeoisement

A (i) The growing affluence of some manual workers. (ii) The electoral successes of the Conservative Party during this period, helped by support from working-class voters. (iii) Some manual workers were buying their own home, becoming more 'home-centred' and were thought to be adopting a 'middle-class life-style'.

B (i) The affluence of the manual workers in the study was achieved by long hours and overtime – their working conditions were still very different from those of white-collar workers. (ii) They did not see themselves as 'middle class', and did not aspire to become 'middle class'. (iii) They were still predominantly supporters of the Labour Party.

Empowerment

1 New Right; 2 obligations; 3 dispersal; 4 negotiating; 5 learning; 6 powerful; 7 right

Equality of opportunity

There are many factors you might have identified, including the following:

1 Some schools have **greater resources** than others, enabling them to have smaller teaching groups and better equipment and facilities.

2 Some pupils do not have English as their first **language**, which is a handicap particularly in the early years of education.

3 Middle-class families are able to provide their offspring with greater **cultural capital** than most working-class families, in the form of knowledge, use of language, equipment such as computers in the home, extra-curricular activities such as music and drama, foreign holidays etc., all of which can give their children an advantage in the education system.

4 Schools are located in different **catchment areas**, and some schools draw the majority of their pupils from poorer homes which are suffering from multiple disadvantages.

5 There are still **fee-paying schools**, so better-off parents can buy a privileged education for their children.

Ethical issues

1 The artificial nature of the environment might place undue stress on participants.

2 The impersonality of the observer/Big Brother raises issues of trust that would be unacceptable to sociologists.

3 The gambling of basic provisions would set unacceptable dilemmas for sociologists, who have a duty of care to those they observe.

4 The potentially unobtrusive nature of some of the surveillance raises issues about the rights of subjects to know when they are being observed.

5 The requirement to wear microphones at all times restricts participants' freedom to choose privacy.

6 The nomination process imposes unacceptable psychological tension on participants, even where voluntary.

7 The removal process can subject participants to intense media scrutiny and even hostile public reaction.

8 Giving such a large incentive would be unacceptable ethical practice, as it might lead to immoral behaviour.

Others may be acceptable.

Ethnicity

1 **(a)** Shared identity based upon a common linguistic, cultural or religious heritage, sometimes, but not always coterminous with racial characteristics.
(b) A view of human divisions based on presumed inherited physical characteristics, and covering large populations of diverse ethnic groups.
2 **(a)** A process whereby an immigrant population is absorbed into a host population on the basis of accepting the host culture as their own.
(b) A process whereby different aspects of different cultures are amalgamated to form a new more universal culture.
3 **(a)** A term which is used to cover a large number of ethnic groups, from Africans to Asian, with some political implications for the solidarity of such groups.
(b) A subset of the black category that denotes a specific geographical and cultural location.

Extended family

1 – B; 2 – E; 3 – C; 4 – D; 5 – A

Family fit

1 Pre-industrial society + Agricultural production, Poor transport, Feudal social relations = Extended family + Home-based work, Geographical immobility, Patriarchal power
2 Industrial society + Industrial production, Good communications, Democracy = Nuclear family + Factory-based work, Social mobility, Greater equality

Family size

1 The availability of effective contraception and the willingness of couples to use it.
2 The economic costs of large families – the connection between poverty and large families has been established.
3 The norms that govern ideas about family size have changed, so that large families are no longer seen as the ideal. The state can have an influence on these norms, through policies that encourage families to have more children or make contraception more available to wider segments of the population.

Family structure

1 – D; 2 – A; 3 – C; 4 – D

Feminisation of poverty

Three possible reasons why women form a disproportionately large group of those in poverty are:
1 Most lone-parent families with dependent children are headed by a woman, and such families are at significant risk of poverty.

2 Despite equal pay legislation, women's average earnings are considerably lower than those of men.
3 Older people are at increasing risk of poverty, and women's longer life expectancy means that a higher proportion of women than men are in the upper age groups.

Feminisation of work

1 **(a)** That women's natural place is in the family rather than the workplace. **(b)** Provides a legitimation for the female homemaker and child-rearer, that is important in society. **(c)** It is a sexist assumption that women are 'naturally' home-makers, and legitimates male power.
2 **(a)** Women balance the emotional cost of going to work against its financial rewards in coming to a judgement. **(b)** Provides an individual dimension in the calculation of security against income by women.
(c) It ignores those women who do not have the luxury of making such a rational calculation in deciding whether to go to work.
3 **(a)** The subordinate position of women in the home corresponds with and reinforces their subordinate position to men at work. **(b)** Introduces the ideology of domesticity as a factor both at home and in work, in dividing women from men in both spheres.
(c) It ultimately relies on a biological view of the nature of men and women, assigning women to the primary domestic role.
4 **(a)** Capitalism needs women to work to keep wages down, but also to take primary responsibility for the home to reproduce the next generation of labourers.
(b) Shows how the exclusion of women from the workforce has given way to the segregation of women in work, in response to the labour needs of capitalism. **(c)** Does not show how men's needs are met under capitalism, in a workforce increasingly staffed by women and where unemployment is increasingly male.
5 **(a)** That women choose not to enter the labour force or take less demanding jobs, because they have a different, less committed attitude to work.
(b) Introduces the idea that women can control their own life-choices and may choose not to work because they are committed to their children's upbringing, without being made to feel guilty.
(c) This ignores the structures under which female and male attitudes to work are formed and the opportunity structures in which choices are made.

Feminism

1 Liberal feminism
2 Marxist feminism
3 Radical feminism
4 Black feminism

First World

1 **(a)** Used to describe the developed countries of the world, which are industrialised and advanced technologically. **(b)** Used to describe the socialist countries of the eastern bloc, which had aspects of First World development, but which also retained features of the Third World. **(c)** Used to describe the less developed parts of the globe, where technology was less evident and poverty more visible.
[The collapse of communism has made the concept of a Second World redundant. It can be used instead to describe the 'tiger economies', which have some well-developed sectors of the economy.]

2 **(a)** Used to denote the least prosperous countries of the world and highlight their lack of development in industrial production. **(b)** Used to describe those countries where industrial production is in the course of 'taking off'. It is a half-way house between developed and undeveloped. **(c)** Those countries that have a strong industrial base and which have generated a great deal of wealth for themselves.
[This represents a linear view of the development process, that ignores the links between the different categories. For example, the dominance of the developed world in global trade may account for the continued undevelopment of the poorest countries.]

3 **(a)** Designates the industrialised portion of the globe, which is mainly but not exclusively concentrated in the northern hemisphere. **(b)** Designates the poorest sector of the world's economies, which is mainly to be found in Africa, Asia and South America.
[While this distinction is largely geographically accurate, it tends to hide great differences between countries in either hemisphere, as well as confusing the position of Australia, for example.]

4 **(a)** Machines, especially computers, which are concerned with the transfer of knowledge in the global economy. **(b)** Tools and equipment that are concerned with providing basic amenities, at low cost and in small-scale projects. **(c)** Very basic machines or tools, that are insufficient on their own to move forward the process of development. They lead to limited industrial production.
[Identifying development only with the technology mainly used in a society is to fall into the trap of technological determinism, which ignores social and cultural factors important in the process.]

5 **(a)** A society in which the main means of production is farming the land and utilising the natural raw materials that grow upon it. It is usually contrasted to developed industrial societies. **(b)** An industrial society in which the means of production are held by private owners, and not by the community or the state. Such societies are dominated by the interests of these owners. **(c)** A society in which the main mode of production is found in factories and offices rather than on the land. This is so, regardless of who actually owns the means of production, private individuals or the state.
[The form of societies in the contemporary world is much wider than these divisions, and in particular, there is no mention of post-industrial or post-capitalist societies.]

Five stages of economic growth

1 – E (iv); 2 – C (v); 3– A (ii); 4 – D (i); 5 – B (iii)

Folk devils

Asylum seekers: 1 Many are claimed to be seeking asylum falsely, as 'economic migrants' not as people in fear of persecution. **2** Pictures in newspapers invariably show them 'behind bars'.
New Age travellers: 1 Claiming state support while travelling around. **2** Untidy encampments left behind.
Punks: 1 Spiky vividly coloured hair sets them apart.
2 Pogoing when dancing – seemingly out of control.
Yardies: 1 Use of firearms amongst rival gangs.
2 Mixed up in drug trafficking.

Formal economy

1 **(a)** Legal work, which is subject to taxation and health and safety legislation, and usually conducted within an identifiable workplace. **(b)** Less subject to regulation and with an irregular connection to the taxation system, often conceived as casual labour.

2 **(a)** Working within the formal economy which is nevertheless hidden from agents of the state such as tax officers, classically associated with the lump in the building industry. **(b)** On the boundaries between legal and illegal working, where declaration to the state is often a matter of personal choice, such as second jobs, or twilight working.

3 **(a)** The 'productive element' of housework, concerned with the reproduction of labour, both physically and emotionally. **(b)** The subcontracting of industrial type work to those located in their own homes, usually badly paid.

4 **(a)** Where services are exchanged within a locality in a quasi-barter system, with limited amounts of money changing hands. **(b)** The interchange of goods and services across the world, supported by vast financial flows between markets.

Functionalism

Some possible criticisms are:

1. The analogy with biological organisms is misleading.
2. The view of people makes them 'oversocialised' and is too deterministic.
3. It exaggerates the degree of consensus and tends to ignore conflict.
4. Societies do not have 'needs'.

Fundamentalism

Fundamentalism refers to a desire among some religious groups to return to the founding principles of their particular religion, which they often see as having been subverted by 'modern' and less religious beliefs and practices. There has been a growth in recent years of fundamentalist movements in Christianity, Islam and Judaism.

Gatekeepers

1. Gatekeeping is the social process whereby news or scientific discoveries are filtered by people in strategic positions, so that only some events or scientific discoveries become broadcast or accepted. The emphasis in the sociology of the media is on the news-values which gatekeepers employ to weed out or headline different stories. In the sociology of science, the emphasis is on the way that gatekeepers use their power to defend the scientific paradigms they believe in.
2. **Mass media:** Setting the agenda for the public debate of issues, by highlighting or ignoring stories. **Sociology of science:** Preventing the overthrow of dominant scientific paradigms and preventing a scientific revolution.
3. **Mass media:** 1 Editors of newspapers; 2 Commissioners of programmes. **Sociology of science:** 1 Holders of research funds; 2 Editors of scientific journals.

Gender

1. **(a)** Women have traditionally taken on the prime responsibility for housework and childcare rather than men. **(b)** There has been some equalisation of roles, with men taking a more proactive part in domestic affairs.
2. **(a)** Girls have traditionally underachieved compared to boys at all levels of the examination system. **(b)** Girls perform better than boys at both GCSE and A level and are making inroads at degree level.
3. **(a)** There are fewer female MPs than one would expect, given the proportion of women in the population. **(b)** Women have achieved the power to vote through their own struggles and achievements.

4. **(a)** Women are more poorly paid than men in paid employment. **(b)** More women enter the labour market than ever before.
5. **(a)** Women have traditionally been represented in stereotypical ways, such as housewife and mother. **(b)** Images of women in the media are very varied and encompass a variety of female images.

Gender codes

1. **(a)** Assumptions about the proper role of men and women absorbed during socialisation and varying according to time and location. **(b)** The way that organisations and institutions encode particular practices about the 'proper' location for men and women in the organisation and the way each ought to behave.
2. **(a)** Used to denote the culturally established ways of behaving for men and women, dependent upon the traditions and ideologies of the society. **(b)** Used to denote the biological dimension of male and female, related to the different functions performed in procreation.
3. **(a)** Established and uniform ways of viewing men and women, in which all individuals of a particular gender are given the same characteristics, regardless of differences. **(b)** Challenges to gender stereotypes have resulted in radical changes in the way that women and men are perceived, and in particular differences within genders have become recognised.

Globalisation

1 – C;　2 – B;　3 – E;　4 – D;　5 – A

Golden age of religion

Secularisation is often judged to have occurred by a comparison between religious practices today, such as attendance at church, and at some point in the past, when people were deemed to be much more 'religious' than at present. This past time is sometimes referred to as the 'golden age of religion'. However, writers such as Hill have pointed out that the evidence for religiosity in this period can be misleading. For example, contemporary accounts from the priesthood are full of complaints regarding the difficulty of persuading the population to go to church. It is also suggested that church attendance used to be viewed as a social obligation rather than a genuine expression of religious belief. Doubt is therefore cast on the existence of this 'golden age of religion' from which we are judged to have declined.

Green revolution

1 – D;　2 – E;　3 – B;　4 – C;　5 – A

Hawthorne effect

1 Interviewer bias
2 Hostility
3 Hawthorne effect
4 Halo effect
5 Prompting

Headlining

1 what they want to read about
2 process of selective exposure
3 news values such as closeness to home
4 what is in the public interest
5 what the main news items of the day are

Health

1 'Morbidity' refers to sickness, whereas mortality refers to death.
2 'Health' refers not just to the absence of illness, but includes physical, mental and social well-being, which are difficult to operationalise and measure. Also, people have different pain thresholds and different views regarding when it is appropriate to consult doctors and report symptoms.

Health care

1 Health care resources and access to health care tend to be distributed in inverse proportion to need, that is, those who have the greatest need tend to receive the least.
2 (a) Some areas have a much higher proportion of doctors per head of population than others.
(b) Some areas have specialist hospitals with the latest equipment, and also provide clinics and 'drop-in' health centres which actively promote good health and healthy life-styles, while other areas lack these facilities. (c) Wealthier people can afford to buy private health care, which usually means that they have access to treatment faster than NHS patients and can also be prescribed drugs and treatments not available on the NHS.

Hegemony

1 Hegemony refers to the 'consent' given by one group to a social system imposed on them by a dominant group. This 'consent' is not natural and spontaneous, but is achieved through the ideological and cultural domination of the subject group by the dominant group.
2 (a) Through the manipulation of the mass media;
(b) through the type of religious belief; (c) through the secondary socialisation process of the education system. These are all parts of the 'ideological state apparatus'.

Hidden curriculum

Some of the things you may have identified are:

1 (a) Respect for authority. (b) School rules laying down how pupils should behave towards teachers.
2 (a) A belief that some pupils are brighter and more 'deserving' than others. (b) Organisational devices such as streaming and banding which group pupils according to their perceived ability.
3 (a) A belief that certain cultures are superior to others. (b) An ethnocentric curriculum which ignores or devalues the cultural background of pupils from ethnic minority groups.
4 (a) A belief in certain values, such as 'good sportsmanship', truthfulness, honesty, good manners etc. (b) A system which rewards the display of these values and punishes the lack of them.

Home background

The educational achievement of pupils from **working-class** and some **ethnic minority** backgrounds is still lower than that of pupils from other social groups. One explanation is that working-class children lack '**cultural capital**', that is, a variety of experiences and material advantages that middle-class parents can provide for their children. Middle-class parents also usually have a greater **knowledge of the education system**, and can use this to the advantage of their children, for example getting their child into a particular school, or getting them entered for certain exams. It is also claimed that **language** is a factor, both for working-class children speaking the restricted code, and some ethnic minority children for whom English is not the first language. It has been shown that high **parental aspirations** can also have a beneficial effect on a child's achievements, and it is suggested that many working-class parents do not have high aspirations for their children. Similarly, **middle-class** children are assumed to be taught **deferred gratification**, where they put off pleasurable things until after they have achieved a certain goal, such as not watching television until after their homework is completed. Home background can also exert an effect in school, as some teachers may hold **negative stereotypes** of children from certain backgrounds, and not expect them to do well at school, therefore do not push them and make them work.

Household

1 (a) Household is all the people who live together under one roof, whether they are related or not.
(b) Family is all the people who are related to each other by blood or adoption, whether they live under the same roof or not.
2 (a) Household economy is the jobs and services performed by members of a family, which might otherwise be done by outside paid workers.

(b) Domestic labour is the jobs and services performed by members of the family, which are not usually given to outside paid workers (though they may be).

3 **(a)** Child-centredness is where the family is focused on the children, in terms of hopes, aspirations, and activities. It stands in contrast to the situation where children were seen but not heard. **(b)** Home-centredness is where the family's social life and leisure activities are based around the home, rather than husband and wife going out with separate groups. It stands in contrast to the situation of segregated conjugal roles.

Human Relations School

1 **Feature**. Paid employment is the main source of identity and locus of fulfilment in an individual's life.

2 **Feature**. Where an individual's essential being and desires are fulfilled, making that person whole or complete.

3 **Criticism**. That the aim of Human Relations theory is to produce 'happy' workers who will work all the harder to make the profits for the owners.

4 **Feature**. Where workers are so committed to the goals of the organisation that they are prepared and are expected by others to work long hours after they would normally expect to go home.

5 **Criticism**. That Human Relations theory does not empower workers but substitutes more subtle means of keeping workers under control than physical or legal force.

6 **Feature**. The situation where the strict hierarchical organisation of work under Fordism has given way to more networked structures, where power is given to workers to make decisions that affect production.

7 **Feature**. Where workers have multiple skills which can be deployed in different ways by the worker to achieve production goals. Workers come together in different combinations of skills depending upon the task to be completed and without the need for strict management controls.

8 **Criticism**. That Human Relations theory is just another, more subtle form of Fordism, as its main aim is the control of workers, to make them more productive.

9 **Criticism**. That Human Relations theory does not foster co-operation as is claimed, but rather the interactions between management and workers are characterised by their lack of connection with each other. Managers do not care about their workers as long as production is maintained, workers do not care about the organisation as long as they are paid.

10 **Feature**. Under post-Fordist working conditions, the power to decide ways of working is said to be given to those who do the actual work, rather than being in the hands of a management hierarchy.

Hyper-reality

1 Baudrillard; 2 images; 3 mediated; 4 representations; 5 masking

Hypothesis

1 Observation: Examination of a phenomenon of interest.

2 Hypothesis: A possible statement of explanation of the phenomenon.

3 Experiment: Testing explanations.

4 Theory: A verified statement that explains the phenomenon.

Iatrogenesis

1 (c); The search for 'counselling' or drugs to make them feel happier, combat stress etc.

2 (b); Natural experiences such as childbirth and emotions such as 'sadness' are treated as illnesses or 'problems' in need of specialist treatment.

3 (a); Adverse side effects from treatment; medical drug addiction; experimentation with new drugs or other forms of treatment.

Identity

1 False; 2 True; 3 True; 4 False; 5 True

Identity construction

1 The family acts as an immediate model for sexual identity, although there is not a perfect transmission from one generation to the next.

2 The law acts as a definer of the boundaries of acceptable and unacceptable sexual identities. As such, it is subject to change and flux as public opinion on these issues shifts.

3 Identity politics movements are influential in shifting public perceptions of sexual minorities, through campaigns and the raising of issues.

4 The power of the 'pink pound' illustrates the way in which patterns of consumption can affect the way that sexual minorities may be accepted in communities.

5 Scientific discourses on sexual preferences influence 'treatments' and the way that members of sexual minorities are perceived.

6 The mass media present stereotypes of sexual minorities that frame their identity. The media may also break down stereotypes by presenting more complex views of sexual minorities.

Ideology

1 Right-wing;   **2** Right-wing;   **3** Left-wing;   **4** Left-wing;
5 Right-wing;   **6** Right-wing;   **7** Left-wing;   **8** Right-wing;

Illness

1 specific aetiology
2 epidemiology
3 episodic view

Income

£2000 of Premium Bonds: Premium Bonds are a form of marketable wealth, while the other two are forms of income. Note, though, that 'savings' are also a form of marketable wealth; it is the interest from them that represents income.

Index of deprivation

1 poverty;   **2** necessities;   **3** afford;   **4** material;
5 household;   **6** social;   **7** nutrition;   **8** lack;
9 majority;   **10** essential

Indicators of class

1 It is closely linked to financial reward.
2 It is linked to status.
3 It is an objective measure, therefore easy to operationalise.

Individuation

1 meaning
2 'New Age'
3 individual; life-style

Industrial conflict

1 **Strike:** A strike is an organised form of industrial conflict, compared to the individual form of the other two.
2 **Mass absenteeism:** Mass absenteeism is unorganised, while the other two are organised by trade unions.
3 **Sympathy strike:** The sympathy strike is illegal in Great Britain, while the other two are legal.

Industrialisation

1 **(a) Feudal relations are destroyed:** The unthinking loyalty and rigid social hierarchy of feudalism are undermined by industrialisation. New, more democratic relationships between people can be formed. **(b) Greater exploitation emerges:** The subordinate classes are subjected to an intensification of oppression, as owners seek to squeeze greater profits from their labour. The few benefit at the expense of the many.

2 **(a) Complex divisions of labour emerge:** These allow a more productive economy to develop. Greater wealth for all is eventually created. **(b) Social dislocation occurs:** As societies industrialise there are massive movements of population. These disrupt traditional ways of living and may lead to anomie.

3 **(a) New products and services are developed:** Innovation creates new forms of leisure and consumption. The quality of life is therefore improved. **(b) Individualism is dominant:** This may lead to an undermining of social solidarity. Increased egoism and selfishness can destroy notions of society.

4 **(a) Rational actions predominate:** The scientific solution of social problems is enhanced. Societies can make progress through the application of rational thought. **(b) Increased bureaucracy:** The development of strict forms of administration may lead to red tape. Innovation may be strangled by rules and procedures.

5 **(a) Greater interdependence:** New forms of social solidarity based on difference emerge. These allow greater diversity and toleration of variety in society. **(b) Increased social control:** Industrialisation leads to greater techniques of surveillance being available. Those dominant in society have a greater potential to control the rest.

Inequality

1 Middle-class people generally have better access to good-quality health care than working-class people.
2 On average, middle-class children still gain better educational qualifications than working-class children.
3 While many working-class people have become owner-occupiers, more working-class people than middle-class people live in overcrowded, insanitary accommodation with fewer amenities.

Infant mortality rate

Possible reasons include:
1 Better living standards, especially improvements in diet.
2 The fall in the average number of children born per woman (declining fertility).
3 Better sanitation and development of disinfectants.
4 Improvements in obstetrics, e.g. decline in use of forceps.

Inheritance

Inheritance refers to the process whereby wealth is transferred from one generation to the next. It is an important factor in the continuing inequality in society in that it passes on to the next generation the privileges conferred by the ownership of wealth, and gives the recipients of inherited wealth a huge advantage in life over those who have to earn everything they have. Inherited wealth is an important factor in maintaining a ruling class.

Interactionism

1 symbolic interactionism
2 the dramaturgical model
3 phenomenology
4 ethnomethodology

Interviews

1 **(a)** Formal interviews are carried out in an official manner to achieve as much reliability as possible.
   (b) Informal interviews are carried out in a relaxed manner to achieve as much validity as possible.
2 **(a)** Structured interviews contain mainly closed questions, with only a few opportunities for respondents to express themselves freely.
   (b) Semi-structured interviews have a balanced mixture of closed and open questions. Open questions often follow on from closed questions and allow the respondent to expand on points made in their own words. **(c)** Unstructured interviews are mainly composed of open questions, with only a few closed questions such as identifying gender.
3 **(a)** Interview schedule is the list of questions that will be asked of the respondent. **(b)** Interview transcript is a written copy of the questions and answers after the interview.
4 **(a)** Standardised interviews are where exactly the same questions are asked of all the respondents in exactly the same way, to increase the comparability of the data. **(b)** In-depth interviews are where the interviewer can depart from the 'script' to follow points of interest fully, in order to gain a deep understanding of the interviewee.

Juvenile delinquency

1 – (d) (e);   2 – (b) (f);   3 – (a) (c)

Labelling theory

1 – C;   2 – A;   3 – F;   4 – E;   5 – G;   6 – D;   7 – B

Language codes

1 True
2 False; language codes are not 'taught' but are learned in the home as part of primary socialisation.
3 False; children of both groups use the restricted code in everyday speech; middle-class children, however, also have access to the elaborated code.
4 True

5 True
6 False; teaching is usually conducted in the elaborated code.
7 True, although the criticism of Bernstein is unfair, as he was not making value judgements about the two different kinds of speech.
8 True

Legitimation

1 The right of kings to rule was 'God-given' – the 'Divine Right' of kings.
2 Leader of the party democratically elected to govern the country.
3 Police officers are given certain powers by the state to carry out their duties.
4 Chosen by the cardinals, who are guided in their choice by God.
5 British society is a monarchy, and the Queen is the eldest child of the previous monarch, therefore the legitimate successor to the throne.

Leisure

1 Leisure is seen as providing an alternative source of satisfaction to work. It makes up for the boredom and alienation of work life. **(a)** For many people work is satisfying and does not need to be compensated for. **(b)** Leisure activities can themselves be experienced as alienating.
2 Leisure is a distinct area of social life, cut off from work and acting as an alternative to it. There are few comparisons to be made between these aspects of social life. **(a)** Much leisure activity is carried out in organisations that are work for other people.
   (b) Leisure is often carried out with work mates, who are a source of friendship.
3 Leisure and work should be viewed together as they increasingly take similar forms and are experienced in much the same way. **(a)** There is increased pressure to work at the expense of leisure. **(b)** People still see the two areas as separate parts of their lives.

Liberation theology

1 Theodicy of disprivilege
2 Liberation theology
3 Theocracy

Life chances

1 **Standardised mortality ratio** – this is a measure of the extent to which the mortality rate of each social group deviates from the average (100) of the age group as a whole. This provides evidence of the increased risk of premature death to those in lower social class groups.

2 **Education** – middle-class children on average still achieve better qualifications than working-class children. Education is a major determinant of the type of occupation, thus contributing to differential life chances in later life.

3 **The 'post-code' distribution of health care** – a way of showing that certain regions and neighbourhoods have much better access to health care than others; in other words, your access to good health care is increasingly determined by where you live. On the whole, poorer regions and neighbourhoods have poorer health care than richer areas.

4 **Type of occupation** – despite changes in the occupational structure, with a smaller percentage of workers in manual occupations, social class based on occupation still reveals significant differences in health. Those at the bottom of the social scale are still exposed to dangerous working conditions.

5 **Housing tenure** – this enables the study of health differences within social classes, and shows that, for each social class, mortality rates for owner-occupiers are significantly lower than for those in the same class group who rent their homes.

Logic of industrialism

1 **(a)** This suggests that all industrial societies adopt similar arrangements for the fulfilling of important social functions, if they are to achieve an efficient industrial state. **(b)** This suggests that societies are moving towards a new set of arrangements beyond industrialism, characterised by being a knowledge society, rather than a manufacturing one.

2 **(a)** This offers the United States as a model for the end result that all industrial societies will resemble. **(b)** This offers an amalgamation of capitalist and socialist societies as a model of how all industrial societies will look.

3 **(a)** This suggests that with the collapse of communism, all dispute about the best way to organise industrial societies is at an end, with the victory of capitalism. **(b)** This suggests that there are three alternatives for societies to industrialise – capitalism, socialism and state-sponsored capitalism.

Lone-parent families

1 single parent; **2** mother; **3** father; **4** housing queue; **5** divorce; **6** state; **7** friends; **8** New Poor; **9** childcare

Loss of family functions

1 The growth of outside bureaucracies does not strip away all of the minor functions of the family. For example, the family remains the front line for treatment of illnesses, not hospitals.

2 It is unclear what the core activities are that remain. While he identified four, others have suggested different numbers of essential functions.

3 While the family may have specialised to some extent, the degree of loss is overstated for ideological reasons. Rather than a specific form of family best suited to an industrial society, the family takes many forms in modern societies and performs many functions still.

Marriage

1 While the number of marriages may have fallen significantly, the number of remarriages has grown. This would suggest that it is not marriage as an institution that is unpopular, but marriage to a specific partner.

2 The pattern of marriage has changed in modern society, with fewer couples staying together for life. A more common pattern emerging is for an individual to go through two or more marriages in their lifetime, as relationships come to the end of their life-cycle.

3 Also known as reconstituted families, these demonstrate the complexity of marriage in modern societies. The relationships in these situations can be difficult to handle, but as they become more commonplace, folk knowledge of them will increase.

4 Though the legal status of illegitimacy has been abolished the number of children born outside marriage has increased. This has caused concern amongst moral entrepreneurs who cite this as a sign of terminal decline in the commitment to marriage.

5 Women have put off having children till later in their lives, so that they can, for example, establish themselves in their careers. This, however, is not a result of a rejection of motherhood, rather it is a function of their control of their own fertility established by effective contraception.

Marxism

1 An explanation of social change which argues that everything that exists (thesis) has an opposite (antithesis) and the contradiction between these two produces a new thing (synthesis).

2 The set of values and beliefs imposed on the rest of society and used to serve the interest, and justify the actions, of the bourgeoisie.

3 Those institutions in society which try to establish the legitimacy of the ruling class by presenting the existing social order as right and natural, thus ensuring the compliance of the subject class.

4 The economic base of society, involving a particular mode of production.

5 A theory of the transition by societies from one mode of production to another.

Mass culture

1 golden age; 2 mass society; 3 inferior; 4 authentic; 5 trivial; 6 negative; 7 low living standards; 8 high tastes; 9 freedom

Mass media

1 **megaphone:** Amplifies voice to reach a larger physical audience.
2 **telegraph:** Allows transmission of written messages across large distances, physically connected by wire or cable.
3 **radio:** Allows voice transmission between one-to-one or one-to-many participants.
4 **television:** Allows transmission of images from one source to many receivers.
5 **satellite communications:** Allows instantaneous global communications.
6 **Internet:** Allows individuals to post messages to a global audience.
7 **digital television:** Allows interactive relationships between producers and consumers of media messages.

Mass society

1 Though the ideology of individualism is powerful in modern societies, people still identify strongly with social formations such as class, ethnicity, region and occupation. This gives shape to modern societies and such groupings also give values and norms to individuals.
2 Intermediate groups such as the family have changed in many ways, but have not declined in importance. They are still the major source of identity in modern societies and continue to stand between the individual and the power of the state.
3 While entertainment is an important element of the mass media, they have a menu of different types of programmes and genres on offer, from which individuals can make choices.
4 The power of the state is subject to changing fortunes. For example, while national governments have become the main form of the state in modern societies, their actions are increasingly constrained by global developments. For example, the actions of the state vis-à-vis their own citizens are increasingly framed within a human rights agenda.
5 Though mainstream media are dominated by corporate interests, the Internet offers an example of freedom to publish any material to any audience. It is simplistic to assume that people just believe what they see in the media – they are aware that the media have a particular line and are often critical of it.

Media effects

1 – E; 2 – D; 3 – C; 4 – A; 5 – B

Media industries

1 economic; 2 postmodern; 3 cultural; 4 wealth creation; 5 manufacturing; 6 Internet; 7 'dot.com'; 8 digital; 9 television; 10 bandwidth

Media representations

1 **(a)** Often represented in terms of a lack of a male role model for the children that will lead to delinquency in later life. **(b)** Lone mothers could be represented as strong individuals, coping with bringing up children on their own, as independent individuals.
2 **(a)** Often represented as either 'camp' (effeminate and lisping) or promiscuous. **(b)** Homosexuals could be represented as including the whole range of human personalities and types.
3 **(a)** Often represented as unkempt and living on the state benefits while enjoying a hedonistic life-style. **(b)** New Age travellers could be shown as freedom-loving, community-minded people who want to be independent of the state.
4 **(a)** Among many stereotypes, often represented in idealised form, with waif-like model figure defining womanhood. **(b)** Women could be represented as being feminine across a whole range of body forms, not just idealised ones.
5 **(a)** Often represented as responsible for their own underachievement in education and for a disproportionate amount of crime. **(b)** Economically and educationally successful Afro-Caribbeans could be represented to demonstrate a range of achievement.

Mediation

1 True; 2 True; 3 False; 4 False; 5 True

Medical model

1 biomechanical; 2 cure; 3 prevention; 4 organic; 5 symptoms; 6 social; 7 mental; 8 environment; 9 episodic; 10 medical

Medical technology

Possible criticisms are:
1 The fall in the infant mortality rate and deaths in childbirth both occurred before significant developments in medical technology. It is suggested that the main reason for the improvement was the rise in living standards and the fall in the fertility rate.
2 Research into the treatment of heart attacks shows that the chances of recovering from a cardiac arrest are just as good, if not better, if the patient is left to

rest quietly at home than by being placed in intensive coronary care units.

3   The significant improvements in the general health of the population which occurred in the first half of the 20th century are mainly due to improvements in people's diet and general standard of living rather than the intervention of medical technology.

Medicalisation

reproduction: there has been a significant growth in reproductive technologies, with the result that for many couples, conception and pregnancy are not 'natural' processes.

childbirth: this is increasingly subject to medicalisation, with mothers virtually forced to give birth in hospital, and often subjected to induced labour so that the baby can be born at a 'convenient' time. A growing number of women are given, sometimes at their own request, caesarean sections.

sadness: people suffering from grief or depression are offered counselling or prescribed anti-depressant drugs such as Prozac, even when there is a rational explanation for their feelings. Sadness is seen as a medical, rather than a natural, condition.

stress: this is a controversial topic, as some medical experts suggest that 'stress' is in fact a healthy, natural and necessary response to certain conditions and situations. Others suggest that what is required is a change of life-style or behaviour. However, it is commonly viewed as a potential illness, and treated accordingly.

sexuality: there have been some suggestions that 'deviant' sexuality, e.g. homosexuality, has a genetic basis, and is therefore a 'medical' condition which could be treated, given improving knowledge about human genetic coding.

Mental illness

1   Definition
2   Socially
3   Males (men)
4   Norms
5   Electro-convulsive therapy (ECT)
6   Szasz
7   Abnormal

Rearranged, the initial letters form the word 'madness'.

Meta-narrative

Theories and ideas which attempt to explain how societies work – also known as 'big stories'.

Metropolis

1   The cities in the Third World that act as centres of First World influence and control. These may be capital cities, ports, trading centres or financial centres. While geographically part of the Third World, they are economically connected to the First.

2   The hinterlands in the Third World, often agricultural, that are exploited for their surplus by agents of the metropolis. Surplus capital thus generated is often transferred back to the First World.

3   Critics of dependency theory suggested that First World agencies did develop areas of high technological development in the Third World that they called enclaves. Mainly based in areas of cities, these enclaves acted as catalysts for development in the hinterland.

4   A situation where imperial rule is established sufficiently so that infrastructure development proceeds in order to ease the exploitation of the colony's resources for the benefit of the colonial power.

5   While nominally free, a situation where ex-colonies continue to be exploited by the previous colonial power, through the establishment of terms of trade that favour the latter. The ruling class in the ex-colonies benefit from these arrangements, which perpetuates them.

Middle class

1   Middle-class workers may be in managerial, supervisory or routine clerical positions.
2   There are significant differences in status between different middle-class jobs, e.g. between a stockbroker and a bank clerk.
3   The large variations in income found in different middle-class occupations result in wide differences in life-style.
4   While many middle-class people own or are buying their own home, others are in rented accommodation.
5   While some middle-class occupations remain highly skilled, others have undergone 'deskilling', accompanied by loss of job security and relatively lower incomes.

Modernisation theory

1   **(a)** When there is 'overpopulation', resources go into remedial action to keep those on the poverty line going rather than being invested in industrial development. **(b)** Many poor countries' resources go to feed the First World with luxury food items rather than feed their own people.

2   **(a)** The lack of sufficient innovators and risk-takers in a society means that it cannot reach the necessary concentration to achieve the 'take-off' needed for development. **(b)** Many of the poor in the Third World take risks every day of their lives and are very innovative in finding ways of surviving.

3 **(a)** Undeveloped societies do not produce enough surplus production in agriculture and basic industries to generate the funds needed for investment in industrial projects. **(b)** Surplus capital is often taken by First World countries or by transnational companies and so is unavailable for investment in industry.

Modernity

1 Growth of the nation-state – state seen as essential to bring about social progress.

2 Development of capitalist economy based on large-scale production and consumption of commodities for the market.

3 Decline of traditional, feudal social order and rise of new social classes.

4 Decline of religion and rise in secular ways of thought.

5 Growing belief in the power of science to explain/change/improve the world.

Mortality rate

Life expectancy is a measure of the average age to which a person can be expected to live. This varies between genders, age cohorts and between people from different social class groups. The **mortality rate** refers to the number of deaths per thousand of the population per year, and is also known as the crude death rate, as it does not distinguish between people of different age groups, which is the age-specific mortality rate.

National Curriculum

Reasons in favour

1 It ensures that all children receive the same basic educational programme.

2 If children move to another area, their education will not be disrupted.

3 It makes it easier to compare the results of tests at different schools.

Reasons against

4 Children mature at different rates, so what is being taught at a given age may not be suitable for some children.

5 It makes it very easy for the content of education to reflect particular political ideologies regarding what children should learn and be able to do.

6 It removes from teachers the ability to make professional decisions regarding the most suitable programme for individual children.

National Health Service

1 This sees the health care of the population as a social service, which should be freely available to all and funded centrally from taxation. It is one of the founding principles of the National Health Service.

2 This means that health care is not dependent on a person's means, but is free at the point of treatment. Controversially, means testing has been reintroduced for some aspects of health care, e.g. prescriptions, dental treatment and sight testing.

3 A report published in 1980 which showed that there were still significant inequalities in the health care and health chances of the population. The NHS was thus failing to overcome the consequences of inequality in society.

4 There have been significant demographic changes since the inception of the NHS, particularly the increase in overall life expectancy and the fall in fertility, which has altered the proportions of people in different age groups in the population. In particular, it has increased the need for geriatric health care, i.e. the health care of older age groups.

5 The availability of private health care allows wealthier sections of the population to buy medical care and treatment. This is controversial in that private patients are sometimes treated in NHS hospitals, usually by staff who have received their training through the NHS. Some medical staff work in both the private and public sector, leading to criticisms that this is one of the factors resulting in longer waiting times for NHS patients, as specialist surgeons and consultants are not available to NHS patients on a full-time basis.

6 A controversial policy which released many elderly, mentally ill and mentally handicapped people from the hospitals in which they had been staying on the grounds that they would be better cared for by their family and the wider community. While many agreed that it was not necessarily a good thing to keep people locked away in institutions, or taking up hospital beds which they did not necessarily need, critics of the programme showed that the support services were not in place, and many mentally ill people have ended up living on the streets. At the same time, some families have found themselves struggling with the burden of caring for a sick or elderly relative.

7 A situation in which the Health Authority becomes a purchaser, buying health care from 'providers' such as hospitals, GPs etc., who bid for contracts. Critics say that this has resulted in falling standards of cleanliness and hygiene as some essential services are 'contracted out', while patients are sometimes transferred to hospitals many miles from their home where the services are cheaper.

8 Patients are increasingly aware of their rights, and are more prepared to complain about what they see as

poor treatment. The worry of possible law suits from patients has led some medical specialists to be increasingly cautious about the treatment they provide.

9 This report, published in 1998, showed that inequalities in health and health care still existed in the population. It focused on a range of socio-economic factors affecting health, and made a series of proposals relating to the health needs of particular groups, e.g. families, young men, the elderly, different ethnic groups.

10 There have been many complaints of the increasing bureaucratisation of the health service, with a growing number of managers, clerks and administrators at a time of shortages of nurses and doctors. GPs in particular also complain that an increasing proportion of their time is spent on 'paperwork' rather than treating patients.

New Christian Right

1 False (The term is applied to several different groups.)
2 False (Christian groups with similar views are found in other countries.)
3 True
4 True
5 False (There is evidence that both Labour and Conservative policies are influenced to a degree by such views, e.g. on the family.)

New deviancy theory

1 (c); 2 (b); 3 (a); 4 (a) 5 (a); 6 (c); 7 (b);
8 (b); 9 (c)

New religious movements

Eileen Barker has suggested that, despite the differences between them, NRMs share the following characteristics.

1 They begin as small, compact units with face-to-face interaction.
2 First-generation members are 'converts'.
3 They appeal particularly to an atypical section of the population, i.e. the young and middle class.
4 They have a charismatic leader.
5 They hold 'unqualified' (i.e. 'black and white') beliefs.
6 They draw a sharp division between themselves and non-members.
7 They are treated with suspicion and/or hostility by non-members.

New social movements

The odd one out is the **Masonic movement**. This is a well-established semi-secret organisation that does not promote any particular single political cause or issue; rather it acts to protect the interests of its members, most of whom are male and many of whom have senior positions in business, politics, the church, the police, the judiciary etc.

New vocationalism

A A belief that one of the prime functions of the education system is meeting the needs of the economy, together with a series of initiatives such as YTS, CPVE, TVEI, GNVQ designed to make school work and training more directly work-related.

B1 No: Maths has always formed part of the basic educational programme.

B2 Yes: Programmes designed to give young people (many of whom would have been otherwise unemployed) basic training and 'transferable skills', with the aim of making them more employable. (Note that such schemes were heavily criticised.)

B3 No: This has always been part of the education programme, although the increased emphasis on these skills is partly a response to criticism from employers about low levels of them in the workforce.

B4 Yes: The idea behind initiatives to increase access to computers in schools is to provide a computer-literate workforce.

B5 Yes: These courses enable school students to study subjects directly related to the world of work.

Newly industrialising countries (NICs)

1 These are oil-rich countries that are not 'in poverty' in the traditional sense.
2 This pair both have strong financial sectors as key components of their economies.
3 These have high growth rates and large gross national products.
4 These have large industrial sectors recently privatised.

News values

2 Locality is important, the more local the better.
3 Celebrities are good news value, as interest is high.
4 Royalty always provide good copy.
5 Stories with a folk devil always sell newspapers . . .
6 Even better with a European dimension.
7 The bigger the disaster the more it hits the headlines.
8 A mystery will intrigue the reading public.
9 Acts of heroism inspire ordinary people.
10 The possibility of a scandal hinted at helps sell.
11 Violence provides a focus of interest.
12 Or anything with animals.
13 Especially if children are involved.
14 Charities warm the hearts of readers.

Norms

1 **(a)** Rules of social behaviour, which define the way that an individual is supposed to act in particular contexts. Norms therefore differ from situation to situation. **(b)** Ideas that are held to have some value for the holder beyond the immediate situation. They provide guidance for an individual's behaviour that goes beyond a specific context.

2 **(a)** The commonsense rules of behaviour that operate in a particular context and which are taken for granted by those carrying out the behaviour. **(b)** A type of power where status is granted to subordinates by superiors, to act as equals in certain respects. It is the acceptance that contains the power.

3 **(a)** A situation where the individual has no rules by which to guide actions and is therefore in a state of uncertainty and anxiety. **(b)** A situation where an individual or group adopts another's norms as a point of reference for their own behaviour.

4 **(a)** A situation where the scientific community has a dominant paradigm that indicates how scientists ought to view the natural world. **(b)** Used by experts in the disciplinary society, to indicate whether an individual's actions are normal or not, according to the standards of society.

North–South

North	South
Great Britain	Kenya
Japan	India
Australia	Colombia

The rest of the countries are difficult to place in such a stark dualism as North–South. Some are 'tiger economies' which have developed markedly over the last half of the 20th century (Singapore, Malaysia, Taiwan, South Korea). Some have aspects of both the North and South within them (Argentina, South Africa). Some are peripheral to the 'North' (Malta, Poland).

The distinction hides more than it explains. While it might have been useful in the past colonial situation, when the countries of the North controlled much of the South, it does not help in a global economy, where the divisions between poor and rich are complex and transnational.

Nuclear family

1 Functionalists
2 Laing
3 Marxists
4 Feminists
5 New Right

Observation

1 **(a)** Participant observation is where the researcher takes part in the activities of the group being observed. **(b)** Non-participant observation is where the researcher keeps apart from the group being observed.

2 **(a)** Unobtrusive observation is both where the observation point is hidden from those being observed so that they are unaware of being watched and where there is no intervention in their activities by the observer. **(b)** Obtrusive observation is where the fact of being observed is obvious and the activities of the observed are directed by the researcher – for example, setting them a task to do.

3 **(a)** Covert participant observation is where a researcher takes part in the activities of a group with no other member knowing they are being investigated. **(b)** Semi-covert is where usually key members of the group know a researcher is taking part because they have acted as a point of entry. **(c)** Overt participant observation is where all the members of the group are aware that one of their members is also a researcher investigating those activities, in which s/he is taking part.

4 **(a)** Laboratory observation takes place in the controlled setting of a closed environment. **(b)** Field observation occurs in the natural setting of the real world.

Occupational structure

1 – 11%;   **2** – 23.5%;   **3** – 14%;   **4** – 9.9%;   **5** – 9.8%;   **6** – 18.6%;   **7** – 12.7%

Official statistics

1 **A** birth registrations
  B death registrations
  C census data
2 **A** incidence of strikes
  B suicide rates
  C crime figures
3 **A** diaries
  B letters
  C autobiographies
4 **A** *Hansard* accounts
  B newspaper articles
  C government reports

Operational control

1 In any hierarchy, senior management determines the structure of the organisation, including how many workers each manager will have under their control. The larger the number of workers under one manager, the greater the span of control. Large spans are associated with organisations with loose controls

over their employees (e.g. where there are many professionals in an organisation). Tight spans are associated with stricter controls over the workforce and are more likely in bureaucratic structures.

2   Within the resources allocated to them, senior managers must decide how many workers to employ to meet their production targets. As this number is likely to change as demand shifts, an important aspect of operational control is the power to take on or sack workers according to the needs of production.

3   Operational control is a form of secondary power because it is subordinate to allocative control, that is, the exercise of operational control is dependent upon decisions already made by those with allocative control.

4   An important aspect of operational control is the ability to manipulate incentive systems to maximise efforts from employees. Performance-related pay is one of the most powerful weapons of operational control as it seeks to balance pay to workers against effort/output. The ability to fix and adjust the levels of p-r-p is therefore one of the main ways in which management can affect the workforce.

5   One of the consequences of having operational control is that those who exercise it have to be prepared to take responsibility for any failure. If targets set by those with allocative control are not met, then it is the operational managers who will likely pay the penalties. That is why the buck stops there.

Opinion leaders

Producers of media messages
1   Intentions of media personnel
2   Encoding process

Media messages
1   Representation of social groups
2   Ideological content

Opinion leaders
1   Standing between media and audience
2   Seen as experts in their field

Local opinion leaders
1   Focus on domestic news
2   Interpret regional news sources

Cosmopolitan opinion leaders
1   Focus on international news
2   Interpret national news sources

Audience for media messages
1   Decoding process
2   Selective interpretation in a social context

Other
1   **Gays** – white males are part of the dominant identities in society, but homosexuals, though more accepted, are still subject to discrimination and seen as different by mainstream society.

2   **Incorporation** – this is where people are absorbed into the mainstream, whereas the other two are processes whereby difference is established.

3   **Roman Catholic** – especially in Northern Ireland, Catholics are characterised as the Other, through their allegiance to the Republic of Ireland. In Great Britain, Catholics are legally disallowed from becoming the monarch.

Parental attitudes to education
Possible answers:
1   If the parents show that they value education and see it as important, then the child is likely to do the same and try hard at school.

2   If the parents take an interest in the child's work, the child is more likely to try to do well. Teachers may also try harder with the child, knowing that the parents are keeping an eye on things.

3   If parents don't make sure that the child goes to school each day, especially in secondary school, the child can start to play truant.

Patriarchy
1   **(a)** The woman has prime responsibility for housework. **(b)** Patriarchy draws upon stereotypical views of males and females that define the public sphere as the domain of men and the private/ domestic sphere as that of women. This is drawn from ideological views of the 'natural' roles of men and women, rooted in their supposed past behaviour.

2   **(a)** The man is seen as the primary breadwinner. **(b)** Patriarchy defines men as 'hunter/gatherers' in the past and therefore they have a biological heritage to provide for the family unit.

3   **(a)** The mother is identified as the main carer of the children. **(b)** Women are seen in the ideology of patriarchy as naturally more nurturing, because of their role as child-bearers. They were thus 'better' at looking after children.

4   **(a)** The husband has the major decision-making power in the family. **(b)** Because the man was identified as the main economic provider in the household, he held economic power. This allowed husbands to have control over aspects of family life.

5   **(a)** The needs and wishes of male children outweigh those of female children. **(b)** For example, the education of sons was seen as more important than daughters, who were expected to marry and run the home for their husbands.

Persistence theories

Changes in mobility have not altered the huge inequalities in wealth and power which exist in society. The gap between the richest and poorest members of society has actually increased over the last decade. There are still significant differences in life chances between members of different social groups.

Perspectives

1 functionalism;   **2** Marxism;   **3** feminism;   **4** Weberian;   **5** post-modernism

Pluralism

Three possible criticisms are:
1   It considers that all groups are more or less equal in their ability to exert influence, whereas some groups are in fact much more powerful than others.
2   'Power' is defined in very narrow terms, i.e. political power.
3   It fails to take into account that some groups or individuals may be so powerful that they can prevent certain issues from ever being debated.

Political culture

1   oligarchic
2   democratic
3   totalitarian

Political identification

British politics used to be characterised by a close **alignment** between **social class** and political party, with the **Labour Party** drawing most of its support from **manual workers**, and with the majority of **non-manual** workers supporting the **Conservative Party.** However, there has always been a significant number of manual workers who voted Conservative, sometimes known as **deviant voters**. It has been suggested that this pattern has broken down, and that **dealignment** has taken place. Much attention has been paid to the loss of its traditional supporters by the Labour Party. One suggestion is that growing affluence has resulted in a process of **embourgeoisement**, by which manual workers increasingly take on **middle-class attitudes and values**, including political support for the Conservatives. Further evidence of dealignment is the increasing **volatility** among voters, many of whom now take an **instrumental** attitude to voting, and change their support from one election to the next.

Political participation

Some possible ways are:
1   by joining a political party
2   by becoming a member of, or forming, a pressure group

3   by exercising the right to vote in elections
4   by standing for election as a councillor or MP
5   by doing voluntary work for a political party, e.g. delivering leaflets, addressing envelopes

Political party

1   It is based on a particular ideology.
2   It has a set of policies which it would implement if elected to government.
3   It attempts to get some of its members elected to government.

Politics

1   power
2   state
3   government

Positivism

Three possible characteristics are:
1   objectivity
2   reliability
3   establishing laws or causal relationships

Postmodernity

1   The idea that there is one all-encompassing explanation for the world. This has been rejected by postmodernists.
2   The idea that the important aspect of postmodern societies is the images that we all consume from a media-saturated society.
3   An image of something that exists as a reality in its own right, but which bears little relationship to real things or events.
4   A feature of postmodern societies that is celebrated by postmodernists, difference indicates the collapse of attempts to mould individuals into acceptable uniformity.
5   The idea that the mass media in a postmodern society have a global reach and so create a cultural identity which is available instantaneously throughout the world.

Poverty line

1   A poverty line is defined as a particular level of income below which a person or family is judged to be in poverty.
2   Three criticisms which can be made of this concept are: **(a)** There is no agreement regarding how the level of income judged to be the poverty line is determined. **(b)** The notion of a universal level of income ignores differences which exist among individuals and which may alter their circumstances, e.g. whether they are a member of a supportive family, what kind of neighbourhood amenities

(or lack of them) are available to them, whether they have access to good, cheap, public transport etc.

(c) The level of income judged to be the poverty line tends to be that which would provide very basic necessities, and makes no allowance for the purchase of other things, e.g. social activities, that most people would see as desirable.

Power

1 group; **2** aims; **3** opposition; **4** explanation; **5** democratic; **6** elite; **7** unified; **8** pluralists; **9** interest; **10** decisions

Practical constraints

1 Theoretical	2 Practical	3 Practical
4 Theoretical	5 Ethical	6 Theoretical
7 Practical	8 Ethical	9 Theoretical
10 Practical		

Pressure groups

1 Promotional
2 Promotional
3 Protective
4 Protective
5 Protective – but also promotional in that it is promoting a particular view of country life

Prestige

1 The concept 'prestige' is rather vague, and may be interpreted differently by different respondents, who may equate it with income rather than status.
2 Respondents' replies will tend to be coloured by their familiarity with the existing situation, thus they may already have a preconceived notion of the ranking of occupations in terms of prestige.
3 Research has shown that people tend to over-rate their own and similar occupations, leading to sample bias.

Primary data

1 by sociologists themselves
2 which is material that already exists
3 primary quantitative data and primary qualitative data
4 structured interviews and questionnaires
5 unstructured interviews and various observation techniques
6 methods decided by the sociologist
7 which perhaps sociologists would not choose for themselves

Primary health care

1 Health care delivered by professionals to the patient/client in the community, usually the person's own home, rather than in a hospital/medical environment.

2 (a) It is cheaper to deliver than hospitalisation.
(b) The patient can usually remain at home.
(c) The 'carers' are likely to know the patient, which can improve both the treatment and the speed of recovery.

Private medicine

1 (a) People should have the right to spend their money as they wish. (b) Allowing some people to buy treatment acts to widen the health gap between rich and poor.
2 (a) By undergoing private treatment, patients 'free up' resources for NHS patients. (b) As many doctors and consultants work in both the public and the private sector, this actually lengthens the waiting time for NHS patients.

Problem of consciousness

1 ideology; exploitation
2 social mobility
3 concessions
4 material

Problem of order

1 – selfish; **2** – peace; **3** – solutions; **4** – coercion; **5** – values; **6** – co-operation; **7** – rational calculation; **8** – optimistic

Profane

1 Durkheim believed that things in society which were 'set apart and forbidden' should be classed as 'sacred', while everything else was 'profane'.
2 (a) The view has been criticised as being oversimplistic. (b) Not everyone would share the same view of what was regarded as 'sacred' in society, therefore what was 'profane' would also differ.

Proletarianisation

Possible answers might be:
1 (a) Many middle-class workers have suffered unemployment and/or are on short-term contracts, with relatively little job security. (b) Changes in working conditions may not affect the subjective class of middle-class workers.
2 (a) Middle-class workers are now just as likely to take strike action as manual workers. (b) There has been some overstatement of the previous skills level of certain middle-class jobs.
3 (a) Many middle-class jobs have been deskilled. (b) On the whole, middle-class workers still enjoy better working conditions and terms of employment than working-class workers.

Protestant ethic thesis

1 Max Weber
2 Calvinists
3 predestination
4 calling
5 chosen or elect
6 conspicuous consumption
7 reinvestment
8 modern capitalism
9 social change
10 conservative

Qualitative data

1 – False, 2 – True, 3 – False, 4 – False, 5 – True

Quantum theory of religion

1 As the theory states that everyone has a 'religious' need, and if this is not met by religious bodies people will turn to other ways of meeting this need, then the growth in 'New Age' beliefs and practices could be seen as evidence of a different way of fulfilling the need for 'religious' experiences.

2 The view does not allow that people may not have 'religious' needs, or that people may believe that there is no world other than the material one. The belief in inherent 'religious needs' is impossible to test empirically.

Questionnaires

1 Not all ages (30, 51–59) are included.

2 This is ambiguous. What does aware mean here? It could mean, I know it exists or I have detailed knowledge about it.

3 This is a leading question. It could also be very offensive to people with AIDS, as it could be interpreted as condemning the victims of AIDS.

4 This is a double question, made worse by the fact that one of the options is a cause of AIDS and the other is not. It makes it impossible to answer.

5 This requires some specialist medical knowledge that most respondents are unlikely to be able to answer with any detail.

6 The question uses technical sociological concepts that respondents are unlikely to be familiar with. While they may have come across moral panic in the news, social construction is a specifically sociological term.

Realignment theories

1 These suggest that old class divisions are disappearing, and are being replaced by other divisions in society, based on other factors which are more important to, or which exert a greater influence on, people's lives.

2 Gender; religious beliefs; housing tenure; urban/rural dwelling; ethnicity.

Relative poverty

Townsend, Mack and Lansley all agreed that the notion of a **poverty line**, i.e. a particular level of income below which people would be judged to be in poverty, was not the best way of trying to discover the amount of poverty in Britain. They chose to focus on the concept of **relative poverty**, that is, measuring people's ability to afford a particular life-style against what was considered **normal** or **desirable** in society at that time. They devised an **index of deprivation**, which was basically a list of goods, amenities and activities, and asked people which of them they lacked. While Townsend devised his own list, Mack and Lansley took a **consensual view of need**, and drew up their list on the basis of the things that a majority of those sampled thought necessary or desirable. In addition, Mack and Lansley asked their respondents whether they lacked certain things because they couldn't afford them, or because they chose not to have them. Only those things which people would have liked but couldn't afford were then counted.

Reliability

1 is validity
2 is generalisability
3 is the correct one

Religion

Religion refers to the organised expression of the perceived relationship between the natural and the supernatural world, with this relationship usually being seen in terms of a god or gods.

Magic is the use of rituals to bring about certain desired ends, whether for good or evil. Such rituals are usually carried out by people believed to have special powers, such as witch-doctors and shamans.

Spiritualism refers to the belief, and the practices which stem from this belief, that the spirits of the dead inhabit a 'spirit world' and can talk to, or manifest themselves to, those still living through the intercedence of a 'medium', who forms the bridge between the natural and the spirit world.

Religiosity

1 Every person has a 'sense of the religious', which needs to be fulfilled by some religious belief and ritual. Religious beliefs and rituals are thus functional both for individuals and for society.

2 If people have a 'sense of the religious' and a feeling of need for this to be fulfilled, it is a 'false need' created by ruling-class ideology. Religion is important in that it can offer comfort to the oppressed and, indeed, disguises the fact that such oppression actually comes from capitalism, not from 'God'.

Religious observance

Religious belief refers to people's belief in some kind of god or spirit with supernatural powers. This may or may not be expressed in some kind of religious practice(s). **Religious observance** refers to activities which are viewed as expressing religious belief, e.g. praying, attending religious services, fasting, going on a pilgrimage, wearing particular garments etc. However, it is not possible to know that religious observance is a true indicator of religious belief.

Reproductive technologies

1   Whether there is a natural 'right' to have a child; surrogate mothers; enabling gay couples to have children; the storage and disposal of eggs; the age of the prospective mother; the rights of biological fathers; the right of egg or sperm donors to anonymity; the use of scarce resources that might be used in other ways.

2   The possible danger of, or complications arising from, some of the techniques; the potential danger to the mother of multiple births; the possibility of passing on genetic disorders or hereditary diseases.

3   Largely because of the moral and ethical issues, this is an area increasingly subject to legislation; the feminist argument is that the processes give men increasing power over women.

Response rate

Scenario 1 – 55%
Scenario 2 – 75%

Although Scenario 2 has the better response rate and is therefore more representative of those the questionnaire was sent to, there are not enough returns for generalisation. Scenario 1, with its larger sample but smaller response rate, has sufficient responses to generalise.

Ruling class

1   Marxist
2   the means of production
3   economic; ideologies
4   rule; govern
5   empirical

Sacred

Some things which are 'set apart' and 'forbidden' are not religious, i.e. certain criminal acts such as incest. Equally, there are examples of religious practices in which the emphasis is on participation rather than exclusion, such as taking communion.

Sampling

1 – B;   2 – C;   3 – A;   4 – D

Scientific management

A   1 control;   2 natural science;   3 profits;   4 experiments;   5 logical;   6 optimum;   7 targets;   8 incentive;   9 piece work;   10 bonuses

B1   There is no guarantee that management will set targets at a reasonable level.

B2   Piece work is about extracting effort from the workforce for minimum incentive rather than providing a fair day's pay for a fair day's work.

Secondary data

1   **News articles** – are concerned with real events, while the others are fictional and give access to the zeitgeist.

2   **Death statistics** – are hard (that is, very reliable) while the others are 'soft' (open to processes of social construction).

3   **Biographies** – are written by someone else about a person, while the others are first-hand accounts by the person him/herself.

4   **Company reports** – are produced by private organisations, while the others are connected to the state.

Secondary socialisation

1 – C;   2 – E;   3 – B;   4 – A;   5 – D

Sect

1   The People's Temple; The Manson family
2   Scientology; TM
3   Neo-pentecostalists

Secularisation

1   Secularisation is generally regarded as the process in which religious beliefs, practices and institutions lose their social significance.

2   Many religious organisations have declining numbers of both members and worshippers; there is a declining number of people getting married in church and infants being baptised; surveys have shown that a significant proportion of people are unaware of the religious significance of Christian festivals such as Easter and Whitsun; there has been a sharp decline in 'Sunday observance', with Sundays increasingly like other days in terms of the social activities that can be pursued.

3   Some religious organisations, particularly non-Trinitarian and non-Christian, have growing numbers of members; when questioned, a majority of the population still express a belief in God or in gods;

other forms of religion such as sects and 'New Age' movements also show a growth; religious programmes on radio and television still attract large audiences.

Selective exposure

1 The **choices** made by individuals as to which newspapers they read or television programmes they watch. These choices are influenced by previous choices made, the social groups individuals belong to, publicity/advertising, **traditional viewing**/reading **patterns** etc.

2 Once viewed/read, the contents of **media messages** are looked at in a particular way. Most often, messages are fitted into **pre-existing beliefs** or opinions, so that the **intentions of producers** may be thwarted. Where messages may successfully challenge pre-existing beliefs, **cognitive dissonance** may result.

3 The process whereby individuals remember or forget **media content**, according to the challenge they may have presented to existing world views. Those messages which are confirming of a **Weltanshauung** are more likely to be remembered in a positive light. Uncomfortable messages may be misremembered or forgotten.

Self

1 **(a)** This is the capability of social actors to see themselves as an external object when calculating the potential effects of our actions. **(b)** This is the capability of social actors to put ourselves in others' shoes to calculate the effects of our actions upon them.

2 **(a)** The idea of oneself, built up by the interactions of others and the way that they perceive us. It is our view of how we think others view us. **(b)** The ability of the individual to think about oneself and one's actions, to reflect on our behaviour and ideas.

Self-fulfilling prophecy

1 No
2 Yes
3 No
4 Yes
Alternative concept – self-negating prophecy.

Sick role

1 **(a)** Temporary withdrawal from certain role obligations, e.g. going to work, caring for others. **(b)** To seek medical help and to co-operate in the prescribed treatment.

2 **(a)** Freedom from 'blame' or personal responsibility for being sick. **(b)** To try to get well and resume role responsibilities as soon as possible.

Signification

1 **(a)** any dairy or food product; **(b)** signifying freshness
2 **(a)** any cleaning product; **(b)** signifying cleanliness
3 **(a)** paper tissues; **(b)** signifying strength

Situational constraints

1 Welfare benefits for lone mothers are relatively low, but going out to work to earn more money can be affected by the availability of good affordable childcare. Even if the children are at school, women in this position will find it difficult to take paid employment other than part-time work, which does not usually pay well.

2 Increasingly, jobs which require few or no qualifications are very scarce, and most jobs now require a certain level of education. The lack of apprenticeships or on-the-job training further hampers the employment opportunities of the poorly qualified, leaving them on welfare or in very low-paid jobs.

3 Despite legislation, many employers are reluctant to employ, or even consider for employment, those with a physical disability, even in cases where their disability would not prevent them from performing the job. Many workplaces are not adapted to the needs of those with certain physical disabilities, nor is some public transport.

4 Evidence shows that the longer someone is unemployed, the less likely employers are to want to offer them work. The long-term unemployed are less likely than other applicants to be offered job interviews.

5 Increasingly, a person's 'post-code' affects certain areas of life. Local employers who recognise a person's address as being on a 'deprived' estate may make assumptions that the person will have undesirable characteristics and would not make a suitable employee.

Social change

Evolutionary ideas suggest that social change occurs gradually, while revolutionary ideas see social change as occurring only after sudden upheavals such as revolutions.

Social class

1 In industrial societies, social classes are usually based on occupation, but only into two broad groups, i.e. those in non-manual occupations (middle class) and manual occupations (working class). Occupational classes exist where occupations have been divided into a greater number of groups, e.g. five or seven, and where there are subdivisions of non-manual and manual occupations, taking into account things such as pay, status, skill level, working conditions etc.

2 The working class is identified either as those in manual occupations, or all those who are non-owners of the means of production. The underclass is a term with no single definition but is usually applied to those at the bottom of the social structure. The American Charles Murray says that the life-style of members of the underclass is characterised by high rates of illegitimacy, violent crime and drop-out from the labour force.

3 These are Marxist terms. A class-in-itself describes workers with sufficient in common to share an objective class description. A class-for-itself emerges when the workers recognise their shared class position and take political and industrial action to change society to further their interests.

4 Proletarianisation refers to the idea that changes in the occupational structure and in the nature of work are leading to non-manual work increasingly sharing many of the characteristics of manual work, and where non-manual workers begin to adopt the attitudes of manual workers. Embourgeoisement is almost the reverse of this process, and describes a view in which increasing affluence among sections of the working class leads them to adopt middle-class attitudes and a middle-class life-style.

5 Class culture refers to the shared meanings, attitudes and beliefs of members of the same social class, which will differ from those of other social class groups. Class interest refers to the fact that some social policies and political situations will benefit members of one class more than members of another class.

Social closure

1 Credentialism
2 Exclusion
3 Solidarism

Social construction

1 **Discovery: (a)** Some crimes are invisible and so never get discovered. **(b)** Some crimes are discovered, but are seen as unimportant by the witness and so go unreported.

2 **Reporting: (a)** Some victims do not believe that the police can help them in any way. **(b)** Some will exaggerate the crime in order to maximise insurance claims.

3 **Recording: (a)** The priorities of the police at any time will influence whether a crime gets recorded or not. **(b)** The area in which the crime was discovered affects whether it is recorded.

4 **Investigation: (a)** Availability of resources determines the efforts put into following up a reported crime. **(b)** The attitudes of police officers will influence the seriousness of the investigation.

5 **Arrest: (a)** Availability of technologies affect likelihood of arrest. **(b)** Notions of 'public interest' will influence a decision to proceed with an arrest.

6 **Prosecution: (a)** Police have alternatives to prosecution available, such as the caution. **(b)** Calculation of potential success will be important.

7 **Conviction: (a)** Juries are unpredictable in their attitudes to defendants. **(b)** Moral panics may influence perceptions of juries.

8 **Sentencing: (a)** Climate of opinion about an offence will influence sentence pronounced. **(b)** Previous history/mental state/personal circumstances of the prisoner affect outcomes.

Social control

1 **(a)** Where everyone accepts the same standards and values as being important for social life. **(b)** Where individuals or groups do not agree or act in accordance with mainstream values or norms.

2 **(a)** Where groups or individuals act in accordance with dominant norms, whether they actually agree with them or not. **(b)** Where groups or individuals undermine dominant values and norms, through words or actions.

3 **(a)** Negative consequences threatened to non-conformists, in order to achieve particular courses of action. **(b)** Positive outcomes promised to those who agree to act in particular approved ways and so achieve social control.

4 **(a)** Obedience to social norms out of a sense of obligation to a higher authority, either religious or secular. **(b)** Obedience to social norms out of a sense of self-interest, either to gain rewards or avoid sanctions.

5 **(a)** Where social control is achieved through the threat of punishment for disobedience. This does not engage the full human being. **(b)** Where social control is achieved through an appeal to emotions and sense of belonging of the full human being.

Social facts

1 thinking
2 external
3 control
4 institutions; behaving
5 reification

Social mobility

1 Social mobility refers to movement up or down the class scale, as measured by occupation, whereas geographical mobility refers to the movement of people and families to different parts of the country.

2 Long-range social mobility refers to a situation in which a person has moved up or down the class

scale by several positions, e.g. from an unskilled working-class background to a professional occupation. Short-range is where the movement is much more restricted, e.g. from an unskilled manual background to a semi-skilled manual occupation.

3 Intergenerational mobility is measured by comparing the occupational class position of a person (usually a male) with that of his father and possibly grandfather. Intragenerational social mobility is where the movement from one occupational class to another has occurred within an individual's own working life.

Social order

1 regularities
2 functionalists
3 cohesion
4 crime
5 predictable

Social policy

1 Sociologists often study the effects of social policies on people's lives.
2 Sociologists sometimes work for government departments and thus can influence social policy.

Social selection explanation

1 Health is seen as a fixed, individual characteristic independent of people's immediate social environment.
2 The explanation presupposes an open society where social mobility is relatively easy.
3 It is difficult to test empirically.

Social structure

1 subsystems; 2 functions; 3 maintenance;
4 positions; 5 norms; 6 expected; 7 socialisation

Socialisation

1 Secondary; 2 Primary; 3 Primary; 4 Primary;
5 Secondary; 6 Secondary

Sociology as a science

1 False; 2 True; 3 False; 4 False; 5 True;
6 True; 7 False; 8 True; 9 True; 10 True

State

1 **Marxist**: An instrument of class domination controlling both ideological and repressive forces.
2 **Weberian**: An independent force operating according to legal-rational rules.
3 **Pluralist**: A partially independent force influenced by different interest groups operating through the democratic process.

Status

1	ascribed	though there would be some problem with transsexuals.
2	achieved	unless you cheated!
3	achieved	
4	ascribed	
5	achieved	though taste and money are also important here.
6	achieved	unless you work in the family's firm!
7	ascribed	
8	ascribed	unless you make a later choice to change.
9	achieved	though parents' preferences play a big role.
10	ascribed	though some would argue that there are elements of choice.

Stratification

1 **(a)** Both agreed that industrial societies were highly stratified, with differences in wealth and power.
(b) Both saw the importance of social class based on the relationship to the means of production.
2 **(a)** Whereas the single most important aspect of class for Marx was the ownership or non-ownership of the means of production, Weber argued that status and political party were also important factors.
(b) Weber's views are regarded as less deterministic than those of Marx, that is, he believed that people were able to change their class position.

Street crime

1 **(a)** Crime is not the result of poverty or unemployment but of the decline in traditional authority and values and the rise of dependency associated with the welfare state. **(b)** Crime is the result of the marginalisation and deprivation of groups, who have little stake in society as a whole. Social exclusion is thus a prime reason for criminal activity.
2 **(a)** Perps are selfish individuals who have no commitment to morality. They have been socialised inadequately into collective norms. **(b)** Perps should not be romanticised, as many in marginalised groups chose not to commit crime but become victims. Perps are those who do not fear stigmatisation.
3 **(a)** The state has a primary responsibility to the maintenance of law and order and therefore must enact legislation and pursue policies which maximise the chances of capture and sentence of criminals.
(b) The state is losing the battle against crime because of inappropriate policing strategies that alienate the very communities who experience most crime. The state must re-establish trust between victim communities and the police.

4 **(a)** There must be policies of target-hardening and increased surveillance of potential areas of criminal activity, coupled with zero-tolerance and increased sentencing of the criminal element. **(b)** The victims of crime must be taken seriously and a return to community policing enacted. At the same time, the causes of crime must be tackled in alleviating social exclusion of the most marginalised groups.

Strike statistics

1 (f); **2** (a); **3** (c); **4** (d); **5** (i); **6** (e); **7** (g); **8** (h); **9** (b)

Subculture

1 Punk rockers used 'anti-fashion' styles to distinguish themselves from mainstream society. This included using bin liners as dresses, safety-pins as jewellery and torn tee shirts. This style demonstrated contempt for the ideas associated with the fashion industry and demonstrated an independence from it.

2 Hippies developed their own concepts and meanings for words, which transformed them from their everyday understanding, for example using 'cool' to describe something that was to be appreciated. Many of these words were used as a symbol of being part of the subculture, especially when drugs were being consumed.

3 Skinheads adopted many values that were extensions of traditional masculine values of toughness and machismo. They were concerned to reject what they saw as liberal middle-class values, which were seen as soft and weak. Their value system has been argued to be a reassertion of a traditional working-class masculine culture, lost in the post-war period.

4 Rastafarians often deliberately provoked mainstream society by advocating and openly smoking ganga, claiming that it was part of their religious experience. The open defiance of the law was argued to be a way of reasserting black identity in a white-dominated society.

Subjective poverty

1 Those things which are regarded as 'normal' by members of a society or group within it.

2 A level of income below which a person or family is judged to be in poverty.

3 The group of people that individuals or groups have in mind when making comparisons with their own life-style or judgements about the things to which they aspire.

4 Being, or feeling, deprived in comparison with another group.

5 The amount of 'social honour' a person or group has in society; that is, the degree to which they are looked up to, or looked down on.

Subjective poverty refers to a situation in which a person or group suffers from **relative deprivation.** That is, while their income may be above the **poverty line,** even considerably higher than this, they consider themselves poor when compared with the particular **reference group** whose **norms** they have adopted or aspire to. While they may not be in any way materially deprived, they will feel a lack of **status**.

Subjectivity

1 subjective; **2** not; **3** not; **4** not; **5** subjective; **6** subjective; **7** subjective

Suicide

1 Aggressive
2 Anomic
3 Oblative
4 Egoistic
5 Ludic
6 Fatalistic
7 Altruistic
8 Escapist

Surveillance

1 **(a)** A characteristic of late modern societies, in which the public and private actions of individuals are watched over. The prime example of this is closed circuit TV in city streets. **(b)** A characteristic of post-modern societies in which the sense of being constantly watched over makes individuals police their own actions without the need for surveillance.

2 **(a)** Used by Foucault to indicate all the ways in which individuals' actions and thoughts can be shaped in particular ways. They were central to a conception of power in post-modern societies. **(b)** Used by Foucault to indicate that the physical body of the individual is susceptible to discipline, so that it is seen as a useful machine, with abilities desired by society.

3 **(a)** One of the disciplinary techniques associated with discourses, in which dividing populations into categories is used as a means of controlling populations. **(b)** One of the disciplinary techniques of post-modern societies, in which forms of examination or testing are used to identify the useful and the less useful.

Symmetrical family

1 This is one of Willmott and Young's stages of the family. This is where, under the pressure of the wife's participation in paid work outside of the home, the roles within the family become more equal, but not identical.

2 This is the process whereby families turn away from the public sphere towards the private. It is seen as a result of the move towards a more symmetrical life-style, in which the family spends more leisure time together, and the greater availability of home entertainment.

3 The fourth stage of Willmott and Young's model, this suggested a move towards greater inequality between family members. It was seen as primarily the result of a greater work-orientation amongst husbands, as demands of employers for commitment from their executives increased.

4 This was the supposed outcome of the discovery of the New Man, who would commit fully to a shared responsibility for the home. The idea is controversial because the New Man has yet to be found in significant numbers.

5 This is the process whereby changes in family life are first seen among the upper classes in society and are filtered down the class hierarchy to appear lastly in the working classes. It was the main way that Willmott and Young saw social change in the family occurring and has been subject to criticism.

Taxation

1 Taxation; 2 redistribution; 3 wealth; 4 income; 5 direct; 6 inheritance; 7 indirect; 8 services; 9 progressive; 10 VAT; 11 regressive; 12 poor; 13 rich

Technological determinism

Technological determinism is the idea that the type and organisation of machinery in factories and offices decisively affects both the attitudes of the workers and the way that work is organised.

A1 Machines are the fundamental factor in the organisation of work in industrial societies, outweighing all other factors.

A2 Empirical research has shown that there are systematic differences in workers' attitudes and in industrial structures according to the type of technology used.

B1 Technological determinists overemphasise the effects of the machines, by ignoring important social factors that also affect attitudes and structures.

B2 Empirical evidence suggests that the relationship between machines, attitudes and structures is much more complex than that suggested by the technological determinists.

Text

Any five from: novel, poem, article, advertisement, film, video, radio, photograph, canvass, song, opera, collage or any other appropriate product.

Theory

A systematic account offered as an explanation of a phenomenon. In sociology, the phenomenon is typically an area of social life or a view of the way societies are structured.

Third World

1 The term 'Third World' acts as a label for the countries of the South, stereotyping them in terms of poverty, squalor and dependence on the North. In fact, such countries have wealthy sectors of the population within them, have many areas of great beauty and can act independently of the North, given political will.

2 The term 'Third World' covers a huge area of the globe and subsumes within it many diverse cultures. Asia, South America and Africa have different histories and therefore have different problems to solve in terms of their poverty. To lump all countries in these continents together is to do violence to their unique situations.

3 By designating these countries as 'Third' is to imply that they are somehow inferior to First and Second World countries, rather than just different.

4 Using the term separates the countries of the Third World from the First and Second Worlds, hiding the interconnections between them that may be important for explaining the dependency of the Third World.

Tiger economies

1 **(a)** Strong long-lasting governments have created social order, so that a stable economic environment is possible. **(b)** Trade restrictions with the developed world have been lifted to stimulate the local economy. **(c)** Governments have encouraged exports to generate capital for investment.

2 **(a)** Authoritarian governments have been unresponsive to calls for change, which leads to unrest. **(b)** The length of time in office has created opportunities for corruption amongst politicians. **(c)** Rapid development of the economy leads to overborrowing by governments and firms.

Transnational companies

1   **(a)** The wealth created by the activities of the TNCs trickles down to the mass of people in the rich countries, through the taxes they pay, so that all ultimately benefit from their profitability. **(b)** TNCs can switch production from high wage economies to low wage countries to maximise profits, thus creating pockets of unemployment in the rich countries of the world.

2   **(a)** The activities of the TNCs contribute to the development of the poor countries through investment in infrastructure and industrial capacity. **(b)** The profits made by the TNCs in the poor countries are not used for developing those countries, but for servicing the needs of wealthy shareholders.

Underachievement

1   **(a)** More girls are more committed to doing well in education than previously, which has put them in direct competition with boys; it is rather the success of girls than the 'failure' of boys. **(b)** The increase in lone parent families has left many boys without an adult male role model, which has led to the increase of so-called 'new laddism' and a lack of discipline at home and school. **(c)** The introduction of coursework in examinations benefits girls, who are prepared to put in more effort than boys at this kind of work.

2   **(a)** Despite comprehensivisation, many schools in working-class neighbourhoods are struggling to counteract the multiple deprivations suffered by many pupils, making it difficult to allow all pupils to reach their full potential. **(b)** Middle-class parents can still buy a privileged education for their children, either by sending them to fee-paying schools or being able to afford the high house prices near 'good' schools. **(c)** Schools in working-class neighbourhoods are more likely to suffer from teacher shortages and to have a high turnover of staff and large class sizes than schools in middle-class areas.

3   **(a)** Racism is still a feature in many schools. **(b)** Some children do not have English as a first language, and will struggle to keep up, at least in the first few years. **(c)** Some ethnic minority groups live in the most deprived areas of Britain, hence educational 'problems' are a feature of wider social deprivation.

Underclass

Characteristics of the 'underclass'

1   A high proportion of people and families living on welfare benefits and a high dependency culture.

2   A high proportion of unmarried mothers.

3   High rates of teenage pregnancy.

4   Neighbourhoods with high levels of violence and high crime rates, particularly involving drugs.

5   Poor attitudes to work and low levels of academic qualifications.

Some criticisms of the concept

1   The groups of people classified as belonging to the underclass are so disparate (lone parents, the poor, the sick, the elderly, unemployed males) that it is not possible to call them a 'class'.

2   Research has shown that there is not necessarily a 'dependency culture' among welfare recipients; many of them are very keen to come off welfare and become self-sufficient.

3   The concept ignores the fact that much of the squalor and blight of inner-city urban neighbourhoods is a result of long-term underinvestment rather than the fault of residents.

4   Many babies born outside of marriage are born to parents in a stable, long-term relationship.

5   The arguments are based on moral grounds, rather than being rational and empirically tested views.

Underdevelopment

1   One example of an industrial sector was the cotton trade in India.

2   Wealth was exploited through direct appropriation or confiscation (stealing from the point of view of the losers) and through taxation to support the colonial administration and to be sent back 'home'.

3   The rules which governed trade were set up in such a way as to disadvantage the goods produced by colonised countries. For example, Indian cotton was heavily taxed, while British cotton was lightly taxed. This skewed the price in favour of British produced cotton.

4   Profits are patriated first through the activities of the transnational companies, whose accountancy systems shift wealth to the First World. A second way is through the operation of trading relationships, such as 'favoured nation' status, which provide for more favourable terms of trade to countries which allow greater patriation.

5   Relationships between the First and Third World countries are the main reason for under-development.

Unemployment

1   **(a)** Government schemes can be used to pump prime job opportunities, turning subsidised jobs into real ones. **(b)** Schemes are expensive and create few permanent jobs, once subsidies are lifted.

2 **(a)** While some jobs may be lost, new higher skilled jobs are created. **(b)** New technologies are designed to save labour costs and therefore reduce job opportunities.

3 **(a)** Globalisation stimulates the world economy generally, this creating more jobs. **(b)** Globalisation moves jobs from high wage countries to low wage countries.

4 **(a)** Left unregulated by government, the market will create more job opportunities, by increased investment. **(b)** The market, unregulated, will keep a high level of unemployment to discipline those in work to accept lower wages.

Unitary elite theory

Possible criticisms are:
1 Just because it can be shown that there are links between people doesn't necessarily mean that they operate as a single unified elite.
2 There is more change at the top of society than the theory suggests.
3 The theory is impossible to test, as even looking at who makes decisions doesn't prove anything, as some people or groups may have the power to prevent some issues even being debated.
4 It underestimates the power of the democratic process.

Universality of the family

A1 Regulating sexual relations.
A2 Arranging for the upbringing of children.
A3 Passing on of property through inheritance.
B1 These functions can be done by other institutions, not just the family.
B2 The variation in family forms is so large that it is difficult to talk about a 'family' at all.
B3 It is difficult to argue for 'irreducible' functions, when, for example, sexual relationships occur outside of the family as well as within it.

Upper class

1 aristocracy; 2 hereditary; 3 land; 4 landed;
5 elite; 6 interests; 7 base; 8 business; 9 wealthy;
10 political; 11 status

Urbanisation

1 – C, 2 – A, 3 – D, 4 – E, 5 – B

Validity

Any three from these possible reasons:
1 It is difficult for any research method to gain a complete picture of the complex interactions that make up society.

2 People's motivations and intentions are difficult to access fully, because sociologists are reliant on the self-consciousness of people, who often are unaware of the reason why they do things.
3 Social situations are subject to constant change, so that even if a fully valid picture was obtained at one moment in time, it might not be valid in the future.
4 Non-sociological factors are important in social situations (e.g. psychological dimension) and it is difficult to establish the balance between them.
5 Because different people will see the same situation differently, it is hard to know if validity has been established.
6 The researcher may have missed an important aspect of the situation without knowing they have done so.

Values

The value-consensus is an assumed state in society where there is general agreement amongst the population on the important principles by which social life should be lived. Without this agreement, social order would not be possible, as conflict over basic issues would be commonplace. Social life is also made possible by the value-consensus as it creates predictability in other people's actions. However, the idea can be criticised for imposing a uniformity upon people, which in reality does not exist. Rather than a value-consensus, there is a diversity of values in society, with struggles for dominance between different sets of values.

(100 words exactly)

Victim-blaming

1 Yes (if sickness or ill-health is seen as an insufficient excuse to prevent the person earning a living);
No (if the cause of such poverty is seen as inadequate sickness benefits).
2 Yes (if this is seen as being feckless and irresponsible);
No (if this is seen as a result of inadequate state family or tax allowance for larger families).
3 No
4 No
5 Yes

Victim studies

1 **(a)** Questionnaires that ask respondents to detail all the crimes they have experienced over a set period of time, whether they were reported to the police or not. **(b)** They show that many more crimes are committed than ever get reported to the police.
2 **(a)** The idea that many crimes are perpetuated against the same people over and over. **(b)** This suggests that location and vulnerability are important factors in whether a person will experience crime or not.

3 (a) The calculation of a person's likelihood to be a victim of crime based on their social characteristics and their routines of daily life. (b) This is important for the calculation of insurance premiums, which take into account factors such as location, age, gender etc.

4 (a) The idea that many victims of crime 'bring it upon themselves', for example, by walking in high-risk areas late at night or provoking physical attacks. (b) This has the effect of shifting the blame for crime away from the perpetuator and onto the victim.

5 (a) The extent to which individuals calculate their own likelihood to be a victim of crime. (b) This is likely to be significantly larger than the realistic chances of being a crime victim.

Wealth

1 'Wealth' refers to the value of all the assets held by someone at a particular time, whereas 'marketable wealth' refers to the value of all the assets that the person could sell if they so desired. For example, some sums of money are held in trust funds and cannot be disposed of, and some people have funds in occupational pension schemes that they are unable to 'cash in'.

2 The answers are:
(a) +3; (b) the wealthiest 25%; (c) 37; (d) 12; (e) 6

Welfare

1 Payment of child support.

2 Increasing the number of higher education places available, and setting targets to increase the proportion of the population going into higher education.

3 Sex discrimination and equal pay laws.

4 Offering flu vaccinations to vulnerable groups; attempting to reduce hospital waiting lists.

5 Winter fuel payments to pensioners.

Welfare dependency

Five possible groups are:

1 Old-age pensioners with no occupational or other pension than the state pension

2 The long-term sick or disabled

3 The unemployed

4 Lone-parent families

5 Asylum-seekers

Welfare State

1 – E; 2 – D; 3 – A; 4 – B; 5 – C

Work

1 driving a bus; busking; teaching in a classroom; cooking a meal in a bed-and-breakfast; reading an official report at home

1/2 ironing a shirt to wear at a meeting; getting the bus to the office

3 teaching your child to talk; cleaning your house

3/4 barbecuing on your garden

4 having a pint; playing basketball

Work satisfaction

1 – C; 2 – A; 3 – G; 4 – F; 5 – B; 6 – E; 7 – D

Working class

1 Working-class people are also employed in skilled and semi-skilled manual occupations. The average earnings of those in manual occupations are less than those in white-collar occupations, although there are wide differences within each group. Fertility rates are now approximately the same for all social class groups; the variations that do occur are more likely to be based on other social factors, such as ethnicity, religion and age of mother at first birth. With the enforced sale of council houses, and the relative affluence of some members of the working class, a growing proportion of them are buying their own homes. There are manual workers in rural areas as well as in inner cities, and rural poverty is a sometimes neglected social issue. Members of the working class read a range of newspapers, including the *Daily Mail* and the *Daily Mirror* among the tabloids, and the *Sun* also has a considerable middle-class readership. The results of the 2001 general election show that just under half (49%) of working-class voters gave their vote to Labour, compared with 57% in 1964. Trade Union membership is in decline, and while there are variations between types of occupation, only about four in ten of those in manual occupations belong to a trade union. While overall educational achievement still shows a class bias in favour of middle-class children, many working-class children do well and continue into higher education, achieving upward social mobility when compared with their fathers.

2 (a) A group of affluent workers identified by Goldthorpe and Lockwood whose centre of interest was increasingly focused on their home and family.

2 (b) A reference to the fact that, from the mid-1950s in particular, a skills shortage enabled some skilled manual workers to earn wages that were comparable to those in some lower-grade middle-class occupations, e.g. clerks. This enabled those workers to achieve life-styles similar, though only in some respects, to those of white-collar workers.

2 (c) A group of working-class voters who historically supported the Conservative Party from a belief that its middle- and upper-class leaders and parliamentary candidates were better suited to governing the country than Labour politicians who generally came from more traditional working-class backgrounds.

2 (d) A reference to a group of manual workers who typically live in the south of England, work in the private sector and own or are buying their own homes. The group was shown to be just as likely to support the Conservative Party as to vote Labour.

2 (e) Also known as the 'traditional working class', this group compares with the former by typically living in Scotland or the north of England, working in the public sector and being council tenants. Members of this group were far more likely to support the Labour Party than the Conservative Party.

World Systems Theory

1 Wallerstein
2 1975
3 Core
4 Semi-periphery
5 Periphery
6 Global
7 International
8 Ownership
9 Marxist
10 Surplus